The Catholic Verses

Also by Dave Armstrong
from Sophia Institute Press®:

A Biblical Defense of Catholicism

—

For further related reading,
see the author's award-winning website:
Biblical Evidence for Catholicism
(http://www.biblicalcatholic.com),
and particularly the web pages:

Protestantism:
http://ic.net/~erasmus/RAZ387.HTM

Sacred Scripture and Sacred Tradition:
http://ic.net/~erasmus/ERASMUS3.HTM

The Church:
http://ic.net/~erasmus/RAZ12.HTM

Dave Armstrong

The Catholic Verses

95 Bible Passages
That Confound Protestants

SOPHIA INSTITUTE PRESS®
Manchester, New Hampshire

Cover design by Theodore Schluenderfritz

Cover image: *Saint Jerome*, by Giotto di Bondone (1266-1336), Upper Church, San Francesco, Assisi, Italy. Photo courtesy of Scala / Art Resource, New York.

Biblical citations are taken from the Revised Standard Version of the Bible (© 1971 by Division of Christian Education of the National Council of the Churches of Christ in the United States of America), unless otherwise noted. All emphases added.

Sophia Institute Press®
Box 5284, Manchester, NH 03108
1-800-888-9344
www.sophiainstitute.com

Library of Congress Cataloging-in-Publication Data

Armstrong, Dave, 1958-
    The Catholic verses : 95 Bible passages that confound
Protestants / Dave Armstrong.
        p. cm.
    Includes bibliographical references.
    ISBN 1-928832-73-3 (alk. paper)
    1. Catholic Church — Apologetic works. 2. Bible —
Criticism, interpretation, etc. I. Title.
BX1752.A765
2004 230'.2 — dc22   2004009805

07 08 09 10 9 8 7 6 5 4

To all those
who have converted from
Protestantism to Catholicism,
especially the ones whose primary reason
was study of the Holy Scriptures

"First of all you must understand this,
that no prophecy of scripture is a
matter of one's own interpretation."

2 Peter 1:20

Contents

Introduction

The total of ninety-five Bible passages presented in this book — as many readers no doubt suspect — subtly makes reference to the famous Ninety-Five Theses of Martin Luther, tacked on the door of a church in Wittenberg, Germany, on October 31, 1517, in protest against certain doctrines and practices of the Catholic Church. That act is considered the beginning of what is called the Protestant Reformation.

The Catholic Church is often attacked (to use a prominent, cynical example) with the claim that it has allowed "traditions of men" to obscure the pure word of God found in Holy Scripture and substituted for it a Pharisee-like tradition by which it diabolically holds souls in bondage, woefully ignorant of the Bible and God's grace and mercy alike.

Be that as it may (of course, Catholics completely disagree with this assessment), when it comes to Scripture, Protestantism is not without its own serious internal inconsistencies, shortcomings, and problems. Since Protestants almost casually assume that the Bible is *their* book — that they have a virtual monopoly on correct Bible interpretation — and that it always supports their positions and disproves Catholic ones, it is good once in a while to turn the tables and closely examine and scrutinize *Protestant* traditions.

The Catholic Verses

No one comes to the Bible as a completely impartial and objective observer or reader. We all approach it, whether consciously or unconsciously, with some sort of preexisting theology, or at least a disposition toward a certain viewpoint. It is impossible *not* to do this. It is part of the very nature of the thinking process.

Protestants are no exception. They claim that the Bible is clear ("perspicuous") for almost anyone to understand in its main outlines (and indeed, Catholics agree that it *is* in many important respects), yet they have been unable, in nearly five hundred years, to come to agreement in many significant areas of theology, and they remain institutionally divided (something repeatedly condemned in no uncertain terms by the Bible).

I shall contend throughout this book that, far too often, Protestants do not take *all* of Scripture into account and that they are guilty of *eisegesis* (reading into Scripture one's own presuppositions) at least as often as Catholics are, if not *more* often. Protestants, especially on a popular level, often emphasize relatively few "proof texts" to the exclusion of a great deal of relevant biblical data.

Moreover, only rarely do they seriously engage the biblical texts utilized by Catholics to support their positions through the centuries. In probably most cases, they are not even *aware* of any passages that a Catholic might use to prove anything that would be contrary to Protestantism. Habitually they do not even entertain the possibility. For many Protestants, such a state of affairs is literally impossible. It is not supposed to happen. When Catholics and Protestants grapple over the Bible and its interpretation, Protestants must always win (so they casually assume).

I hasten to add — and emphasize to the greatest degree — that these tendencies of bias and subjectivism and subconscious influence of denominational traditions do not necessarily entail a deliberate attempt to ignore or to twist Scripture. Every serious student of the Bible comes to the biblical text with a theological framework, in order to interpret it and make sense of it in its entirety. This is proper and right, and no one should have any objection to it.

Both Catholics and Protestants engage in systematic theology, a method that involves finding proof texts for a given doctrine. In so doing, men will have honest disagreements, in good faith. We highly respect the devotion to Bible study and to theological reflection exhibited by many of our Protestant brethren — often putting Catholics to shame.

With that disclaimer always in mind, and without at all questioning the sincerity or integrity of Protestants, I shall now proceed to offer a critique of common Protestant attempts to ignore, explain away, rationalize, wish away, overpolemicize, minimize, de-emphasize, evade clear consequences of, or special plead with regard to "the Catholic Verses": ninety-five biblical passages that provide the foundation for Catholicism's most distinctive doctrines. This is not a scholarly work, as I am no scholar in the first place, but merely a lay Catholic apologist; but it is not "anti-scholarly," and I will incorporate scholarship wherever necessary to substantiate the argument.

My emphasis will be on the popular level, but John Calvin and Martin Luther (the primary founders of Protestantism, or, as Protestants and historians refer to them, "Reformers") will be cited quite frequently, as well as other scholars, especially well-known Protestant commentators such as Matthew Henry, John Wesley, Albert Barnes, and Adam Clarke, when a particular argument concerning the prevalent Protestant viewpoint vis-à-vis a Bible passage needs to be backed up or documented.

I will cite Martin Luther and John Calvin primarily as "prototypes" for later Protestant exegesis and hermeneutics (fancy words for Bible commentary and interpretation). In other words, their commentary will serve as representative of Protestantism, insofar as they hold to historically influential positions that are largely held by subsequent and current-day Protestants. Most Protestants respect these two men, even if they deny (as surprisingly many do) any direct or significant historical and theological connection with them.

Occasionally, however, I will cite these men for the opposite reason: to demonstrate how Luther or Calvin, or both, held to views that are *rejected* by today's Protestants. In some cases (such as the issue of contraception), it is striking how early Protestant opinion was virtually identical to traditional Catholic beliefs. These are instances in which, ironically, Protestants today are far less in harmony with their own historical and theological heritage than Catholics are, and where today's Protestants ignore or reinterpret some Bible passages in ways that would have been utterly rejected by the founders of Protestantism. A few historically significant examples of this sort will be included in this book for educational purposes and illustrate that Protestant theology is a fluid, changeable phenomenon.

I will assert — with all due respect and, I hope, with a minimum of "triumphalism" — the ultimate incoherence, inadequacy, inconsistency, or exegetical and theological implausibility of the Protestant interpretations, and will submit the Catholic views as exegetically and logically superior alternatives.

The ninety-five Catholic Verses here considered are, I submit, so closely related to Catholic "distinctives" that they form an essential body of biblical material, useful and crucial for every Catholic who wishes to better understand and defend the Catholic Faith. Nothing is more effective (or more respected), in discourse with our Protestant brothers and sisters in the Lord than a cogent, persuasive biblical argument.

It should also be noted how the explosion of religious dialogue on the Internet has been a great and exciting opportunity for expanding discussions like these. One might describe theologically oriented Internet discussion boards, lists, and chat rooms as the twenty-first-century equivalent of Speaker's Corner in London's Hyde Park, a place where Catholics (for example, the well-known lay apologist Frank Sheed and his Catholic Evidence Guild) disputed and dialogued with atheists, Protestants, and other opponents of Catholicism, and where free discussion occurred. I have been very active in online apologetics for nearly eight years and will incorporate in this book my experiences in discussing Scripture with Protestants.[1]

As always in my apologetics, I ask readers to have an open mind and to be as objective as possible in their appraisal of competing points of view. I ask (in fact, plead with) non-Catholic readers to allow the Catholic outlook a fair hearing. Perhaps many will be surprised to see that Catholicism can be so strongly supported by the Bible.

It is one thing to have an honest disagreement with a fellow Christian without questioning his basic integrity or the worth of his paradigm or theological framework or tradition; it is quite another to reject other Christian theologies and belief systems as corrupt, "unbiblical" entities that can succeed only by a deliberately dishonest distortion or outright suppression of the biblical text. Too often the latter approach is wrongly applied to Catholicism by Protestants.

Catholics typically do not respond in kind; we gladly acknowledge Protestants as fellow Christians and brothers and sisters in

---

[1] The Second Vatican Council dealt with the use of such means in its Decree on the Means of Social Communication (*Inter Mirifica:* 4 December 1963), referring to "those means of communication which of their nature can reach and influence . . . the whole of human society. These are the press, the cinema, radio, television, and others of a like nature" (1). The council urged that all Catholics "should make a concerted effort to ensure that the means of communication are put at the service of the multiple forms of the apostolate without delay and as energetically as possible" (13).

Christ and rejoice in the many things that we hold in common. One can disagree without belittling the opponents' belief system or demonizing them as individuals. That is my present goal: I consider this discussion an "in-house" fight, not a battle between darkness and light or good and evil. I write as a fellow brother in Christ with a respectful disagreement.

If this book can convince the reader that Catholicism is at least as "biblically respectable" as any brand of Protestantism, I will have succeeded in my goal. In any event, I trust that all students of the Bible will be interested in comparative exegesis and a side-by-side analysis of competing views. Of course, my ultimate aim is persuasion, but increased understanding (even while disagreement remains) is also a worthy accomplishment.

The Bible is our common ground, and I hope we can all engage in mutually respectful discussion of its contents and meaning. I learned to love and study holy Scripture as a Protestant, and for that (among many other blessings) I shall always be thankful.

Finally, I wish to address an anticipated charge that I am merely "proof-texting" or operating in a "Protestant" mode of *sola Scriptura*, whereby every doctrine must be explicitly proven in Scripture, and in Scripture alone. Catholics do not believe that. We do believe, however, that all our doctrines are present in Scripture, either explicitly or in kernel form (later to be more fully developed), or as straightforward deductions from biblical material. This is the notion of the "material sufficiency" of Scripture.

Nevertheless, not every doctrine has to rest solely on Scripture. All doctrines need to be *harmonious* with, and not *contradictory* to, Scripture (which is a notion distinct from *sola Scriptura*). Another way to look at this difference is to realize that when a Protestant uses the terms *unbiblical* or *extrabiblical,* he usually means "not found in Scripture." When Catholics, however, use those terms, we mean "not explicitly in Scripture, yet not contrary to it, and fully consistent with it (as all true doctrines must be)."

I recently dealt with this very charge, made by an Orthodox Christian who suggested that I was adopting the Protestant method in my biblical apologetics. I emphasized to him that when Catholics argue from Scripture, we are acting very much like the Church Fathers, who constantly appealed to Scripture against the heretics, but whose final court of appeal was always Tradition and Holy Mother Church, where the proper interpretation of Scripture was verified. Like St. Athanasius in his dealing with the Arian heretics (who denied that Jesus was God), we can (and it is very good to) argue mostly from Scripture, but rest our final appeal on the Church and unbroken apostolic Tradition.

In effect, Catholics are saying, "So you want to argue doctrines based on the standard of Bible alone? We can match you verse for verse (without adopting your principle of *sola Scriptura*). We aren't afraid to subject our views to the most intense biblical scrutiny and exegesis. In fact, we eagerly welcome it." The fact remains that diverse interpretations arise, and a final authority outside of Scripture is needed to resolve those controversies. This does not imply in the least that Scripture itself (rightly understood) is not sufficient to overcome the errors. It is only *formally* insufficient by itself (that is, it cannot interpret itself; this is where Church and Tradition come in).

Needless to say (but I want to make it clear!): my arguments are not the be-all and end-all of theological reflection or even of the specific field of apologetics. I offer them as food for thought; as a perspective, I believe, entirely in accord with the dogmatic teachings of the Church. My main purpose is to show that Catholics need not "yield" Scripture to Protestants, as if the Bible were a Protestant book. It is not. It is, if we must speak in this fashion, a Catholic book, produced and preserved by Catholics for nearly 1,500 years before Protestantism even appeared.

The Bible translation used in this book is the Revised Standard Version (RSV; Old Testament: 1952; New Testament: second edition, 1971). I have deliberately refrained from using the Catholic edition of the RSV (RSVCE) to avoid any charges of stacking the deck in favor of Catholic interpretation. Certain instances where the RSVCE translation differs will be mentioned in the text.

The Catholic Verses

Chapter One

The Church

THE CHURCH IS THE "PILLAR OF THE TRUTH"

1 Timothy 3:15: ". . . the household of God, which is the church of the living God, the pillar and bulwark of the truth."

Catholics accept this passage at face value: the Church is the ground or *foundation* (the word used in the New International Version [NIV] translation) of truth; it is infallible; it is specially protected by the Holy Spirit so that it can be the Guardian and Preserver of apostolic tradition and truth and doctrine.

Protestants (in the final analysis) do not believe this, which is the reason they refer far more often to "scriptural authority" than to "Church authority" (as if the two were opposed to each other). Catholics, on the other hand, believe in faith that they *will not* and *cannot* be in conflict.

This verse, then, would seem to run counter to the foundational assumption of Protestantism: *sola Scriptura*, or "Scripture alone," which is the formal principle of authority of Protestantism. *Sola Scriptura* holds that no institutional Church is infallible. A church is doctrinally correct only insofar as it can be backed up by Scripture (as ultimately interpreted by Joe Q. Protestant, however, which is the rub). Martin Luther graphically expresses the Protestant view of authority:

> The Pope, Luther, Augustine, Paul, or even an angel from Heaven — these should not be masters, judges, or arbiters but only witnesses, disciples, and confessors of Scripture (in Althaus, 75; LW, 26, 58).

In a 1538 sermon, Luther proclaimed:

> No one likes to say that the church is in error; if the church teaches anything in addition to or contrary to God's word, we must say that it is in error (in Althaus, 336; LW, 26, 66 ff.).

To distance himself from the Catholic view, Luther (reluctantly, as indicated elsewhere) eventually modified his definition of the Church. The true Church, he said, was "hidden," and not always synonymous with an official, visible, institutional church. This "church" cannot err in the faith at all. Indeed, Luther applied 1 Timothy 3:15 literally to this invisible church, as he envisioned it (see Althaus, 342).

And thus the stage was set for the ambiguous ecclesiology that has been a difficulty of the Protestant position ever since. Reluctant to acknowledge the Catholic Church headed by the Pope in Rome, Protestants must fall back on an alternate notion of an invisible, spiritual church that cannot be identified in earthly, historical, concrete terms.

The most thoughtful, historically knowledgeable Protestants wish to maintain a semblance of church authority and authoritative tradition (always subservient to Scripture, of course), but are unable to do so coherently, having knocked out the very "pillar and ground" of that authority (as Scripture describes) and replaced it with the supremacy of individual private judgment. According to *sola Scriptura*, the Protestant is ultimately free to pick and choose his doctrines in a sort of "cafeteria Christianity" — so long as he can reconcile them with his own interpretation of Scripture.

Luther thought that the Catholic Church retained true elements; therefore, for him the universal church was not merely "a Platonic ideal" (as Althaus puts it). But the individual believer, led by the Holy Spirit and the self-interpreting, perspicuous Scripture can and should judge it where it has gone wrong.

John Calvin argues that "the truth, instead of being extinguished in the world, remains unimpaired" because believers have "the Church as a faithful guardian, by whose aid and ministry it is maintained" (*Institutes*, IV, 8, 12). But because Calvin disagrees with the theology of the Catholic Church (and casually assumes the prerogative to judge that Church), he manages to believe that it "died" and that somehow a "new church" (of course, the one he advocates) has arisen to take its place:

> [I]f the true Church is "the pillar and ground of the truth" (1 Tim. 3:15), it is certain that there is no Church where lying and falsehood have usurped the ascendancy (*Institutes*, IV, 2, 1).

For Calvin, it is undeniably true that the Catholic Church has become hopelessly corrupt, and he freely applies to it terms such as "perverted," "lies," "foulest sacrilege," "intolerable superstitions," "idolatry and impiety," and "wickedness" (*Institutes*, IV, 2, 2). Thus, it cannot possibly be the church referred to in 1 Timothy 3:15.

In his *Institutes* (IV, 2, 10), Calvin argues that the "church" is indeed the "pillar of the truth" and has the "power of the keys," but since Rome is "contaminated by idolatry, superstition, and impious doctrine" it is clearly not *the* Church: "They either are not churches, or no badge will remain by which the lawful meetings of the faithful can be distinguished from the meetings of Turks." Although at first he seemed to agree with and endorse the idea that the Church is the foundation of the truth, Calvin eventually collapses back onto the principle of private judgment. In other words, the Church is the pillar of the truth unless one judges that it is not.

Almost by logical necessity, then, Calvin too must appeal to an *invisible church*, a concept not taught in Scripture at all:

> Often, too, by the name of Church is designated the whole body of mankind scattered throughout the world, who profess to worship one God and Christ . . . it is necessary to believe the invisible Church, which is manifest to the eye of God only (*Institutes*, IV, 1, 7).

Some of the inherent problems of this approach will be dealt in the chapter on divisions and denominationalism. But this passage continues to pose problems for Protestants in other ways. Methodist commentator Adam Clarke, in his commentary, illustrates Protestant confusion and mixed feelings over this seemingly easily understood verse:

> Never was there a greater variety of opinions on any portion of the sacred Scripture than [there] has been on this and the following verse. . . . It would be almost impossible, after reading all that has been said on this passage, for any man to make up his own mind.

He proceeds to outline four theories. One option is that the phrase refers to the Church. The others are Timothy, the mystery of godliness, and God himself.

The Catholic, of course, is not burdened by these internal inconsistencies and the need to special plead (and adopt desperate explanations) in order to disagree with one particular view at all costs. Catholics do not have to pit the Bible against the Church or deny that God is able to preserve his truth in a visible, institutional Church.

We agree with these eloquent words from the famous Trappist monk Thomas Merton:

[T]he truth is that the saints arrived at the deepest and most vital and also the most individual and personal knowledge of God precisely *because* of the Church's teaching authority, precisely through the tradition that is guarded and fostered by that authority (Merton, 81).

THE BINDING AUTHORITY OF
COUNCILS, LED BY THE HOLY SPIRIT

Acts 15:28-29: "For it has seemed good to the Holy Spirit and to us to lay upon you no greater burden than these necessary things: that you abstain from what has been sacrificed to idols and from blood and from what is strangled and from unchastity. If you keep yourselves from these, you will do well. Farewell."

Acts 16:4: "As they went on their way through the cities, they delivered to them for observance the decisions which had been reached by the apostles and elders who were at Jerusalem."

These passages offer a proof that the early Church held to a notion of the infallibility of Church councils, and to a belief that they were especially guided by the Holy Spirit (precisely as in Catholic Church doctrine concerning ecumenical councils). Accordingly, Paul takes the message of the conciliar decree with him on his evangelistic journeys and preaches it to the people. The Church had real authority; it was binding and infallible.

This is a far cry from the Protestant principle of *sola Scriptura*, which presumes that councils and popes can err and thus need to be corrected by Scripture. Popular writer and radio expositor R. C. Sproul expresses the standard Evangelical Protestant viewpoint on Christian authority:

> For the Reformers, no church council, synod, classical theologian, or early church father is regarded as infallible. All are open to correction and critique (in Boice, 109).

Arguably, this point of view derives from Martin Luther's stance at the Diet of Worms in 1521 (which might be construed as the formal beginning of the formal principle of authority in Protestantism: *sola Scriptura*). Luther passionately proclaimed:

> Unless I am convicted by Scripture and plain reason — I do not accept the authority of popes and councils, for they have contradicted each other — my conscience is captive to the Word of God. I cannot and I will not recant anything, for to go against conscience is neither right nor safe. God help me, Amen. Here I stand. I cannot do otherwise (in Bainton, 144).

A Protestant might reply that since this Council of Jerusalem referred to in Acts consisted of apostles, and since an apostle proclaimed the decree, both possessed a binding authority that was later lost (as Protestants accept apostolic authority as much as Catholics do). Furthermore, the incidents were recorded in inspired, infallible Scripture. They could argue that none of this is true of later Catholic councils; therefore, the attempted analogy is null and void.

But this is a bit simplistic, since Scripture is our model for everything, including Church government, and all parties appeal to it for their own views. If Scripture teaches that a council of the Church is authoritative and binding, it is implausible and unreasonable to assert that no future council can be so simply because it is not conducted by apostles.

Scripture is our model for doctrine and practice (nearly all Christians agree on this). The Bible does not exist in an historical vacuum, but has import for the day-to-day life of the Church and Christians for all time. St. Paul told us to imitate him (e.g., 2 Thess. 3:9). And he went around proclaiming decrees of the Church. No one was at liberty to disobey these decrees on the grounds of conscience, or to declare by "private judgment" that they were in error (per Luther).

It would be foolish to argue that the way the Apostles conducted the governance of the Church has no relation whatsoever to how later Christians engage in the same task. It would seem rather obvious that Holy Scripture assumes that the model of holy people (patriarchs, prophets, and apostles alike) is to be followed by Christians. This is the point behind entire chapters, such as, notably, Hebrews 11.

When the biblical model agrees with their theology, Protestants are all too enthusiastic to press their case by using scriptural examples. The *binding authority* of the Church was present here, and there is no indication whatever that anyone was ever allowed to dissent from it. That is the fundamental question. Catholics wholeheartedly agree that no new Christian doctrines were handed down after the Apostles. Christian doctrine was present in full from the beginning; it has only organically developed since.

John Calvin has a field day running down the Catholic Church in his commentary for Acts 15:28. It is clear that he is uncomfortable with this verse and must somehow explain it in Protestant terms. But he is not at all unanswerable. The fact remains that the decree was made, and it was binding. It will not do (in an attempt to undercut ecclesial authority) to proclaim that this particular instance was isolated. For such a judgment rests on Calvin's own completely arbitrary authority, which he claims but cannot prove. Calvin merely states his position, rather than *arguing* it, in the following passage:

[I]n vain do they go about out of the same to prove that the Church had power given to decree anything contrary to the word of God. The Pope hath made such laws as seemed best to him, contrary to the word of God, whereby he meant to govern the Church.

This strikes me as somewhat desperate. First, Catholics have never argued that the Pope has power to make decrees contrary to the Bible (making Calvin's slanderous charge a straw man). Calvin goes on to use vivid language, intended to resonate with already strong emotions and ignorance of Catholic theology. It is an old lawyer's tactic: when one has no case, attempt to caricature the opponent, obfuscate, and appeal to emotions rather than to reason.

Far more sensible and objective are the comments on Acts 15:28 and 16:4 from the Presbyterian scholar Albert Barnes in his famous *Barnes's Notes* commentary:

For it seemed good to the Holy Ghost. This is a strong and undoubted claim to inspiration. It was with special reference to the organization of the church that the Holy Spirit had been promised to them by the Lord Jesus, Matthew 18:18-20; John 14:26.

In this instance, it was the decision of the council in a case submitted to it; and it implied an obligation on the Christians to submit to that decision.

Barnes actually acknowledges that the passage has some implication for ecclesiology in general. It is remarkable, on the other hand, that Calvin seems concerned about the possibility of a group of Christians — in this case, a council — being led by the Holy Spirit to achieve a true doctrinal decree, whereas he has no problem with the notion that *individuals* can achieve such certainty:

[O]f the promises which they are wont to allege, many were given not less to private believers than to the whole Church [cites Matthew 28:20, John 14:16-17]. . . . We are not to give permission to the adversaries of Christ to defend a bad cause, by wresting Scripture from its proper meaning (*Institutes*, IV, 8, 11).

But it will be objected that whatever is attributed in part to any of the saints, belongs in complete fullness to the Church. Although there is some semblance of truth in this, I deny that it is true (*Institutes*, IV, 8, 12).

Calvin believes that Scripture is self-authenticating. I appeal, then, to the reader to judge the preceding passages. Do they seem to support the notion of an infallible Church council (apart from the question of whether the Catholic Church, headed by the Pope, is that Church)? Do Calvin's arguments succeed? For Catholics, the import of Acts 15:28 is clear and undeniable.

THE AUTHORITY OF ORAL TRADITION

2 Timothy 1:13-14: "Follow the pattern of the sound words which you have heard from me, in the faith and love which are in Christ Jesus; guard the truth that has been entrusted to you by the Holy Spirit who dwells within us."

2 Timothy 2:2: "And what you have heard from me before many witnesses entrust to faithful men who will be able to teach others also."

Jude 3: "Beloved, being very eager to write to you of our common salvation, I found it necessary to write appealing to you to contend for the faith which was once for all delivered to the saints."

> **Acts 2:42:** "And they devoted themselves to the apostles' teaching and fellowship, to the breaking of bread and the prayers."

Catholics believe that these verses clearly set forth a notion of a binding oral tradition that has as much authority as the written word of Scripture. Protestants also believe in the notion of a set of doctrines received and handed down by the Apostles, and that they are the legatees of that deposit, which is preserved infallibly in inspired Scripture. But they deny that there is one institutional, infallible Church ordained by God to preserve the doctrine inviolate down through history. Many Protestants will even freely admit that they do not think any one Christian group (including their own chosen one) "gets it all right."

It seems to be inconceivable to most Protestants (this was true in my case, in former years) that any human institution could be protected by God to such an extraordinary degree. It certainly takes faith to believe such a thing, but the notion is not contrary to anything in Holy Scripture, and is, arguably, indicated in the Bible in more than one place, including the above passages.

The oral, spoken component of 2 Timothy 1:13-14 and 2:2 is also noteworthy (and potentially troubling to Protestants). St. Paul seems to make no distinction between written and oral teaching. He considers both equally authoritative (and able to be "guarded by" or "entrusted" to men).

The usual Protestant argument I have encountered when bringing up this topic has been to assert that this apostolic deposit was authoritatively contained and summarized in the Bible, and nowhere else. Thus, so they tell us, we can dismiss extrabiblical "claimants" as unnecessary for the preservation of Christian truth. It is all in the Bible.

Apart from vexing problems of *biblical interpretation*, this reply fails to take into account the fact that none of the four passages just cited even *mentions* the Bible in this regard. That does not mean that the Bible would not play a large (if not primary) role in such preservation, but it certainly suggests that nonbiblical aspects cannot be so cavalierly dismissed. The oral tradition St. Paul refers to would appear to rule that out in and of itself.

Adam Clarke uses his commentary on 2 Timothy 2:2 merely to rant (in most unscholarly fashion) against apostolic succession (thus suggesting that he had nothing constructive to say about it):

> But where is the uninterrupted apostolical succession! Who can tell? Probably it does not exist on the face of the world. All the pretensions to it by certain Churches are as stupid as they are idle and futile.

The Calvinist Charles Spurgeon, preaching on 2 Timothy 1:13, in his sermon "The Form of Sound Words," delivered on May 11, 1856, obviously does not think that true doctrine could be preserved by a visible Church and accepts the unbiblical idea of *defectibility*: that a true Church could fall away from God's truth. Spurgeon rejects the very notion of a true Christian tradition and the historical sense of doctrinal continuity. Rather than follow the Pauline injunction to follow oral tradition, Spurgeon advises his hearers to give no heed to traditions that have been passed down. This is because, he says, the Catholic Church was formerly a Christian Church but then became corrupted little by little until it no longer was.

Of course, no reason is given for this belief. That the Catholic Church is corrupt and compromised beyond all hope is part of classical Protestant mythology. It need not be argued; it is assumed and is common "knowledge" in certain anti-Catholic Protestant circles.

Rather than engage in an ahistorical polemic against apostolic succession and Rome, John Henry Newman, while still an Anglican, was able to interpret Acts 2:42 in a vastly different way. He grounds the notion in easily understood Bible passages that refer to following the Apostles:

> He had said to all the Apostles before His resurrection, "Whatsoever ye *shall* bind on earth, shall be bound in heaven"; the time was not yet come; but after it, He said, "As my Father hath sent me, even so send I you" [Matthew 18:18; John 20:21]. Then He *did* what before He promised; henceforth all men must join themselves to the Apostles, which they were not told to do before. Accordingly, we read in the second chapter of the Acts that those who were converted and baptized, "continued steadfastly in the Apostles' doctrine" — but not only doctrine; it was not enough to preach and hold the same doctrine as they, but it is added, in the Apostles' "fellowship" — they "continued steadfastly in the Apostles' doctrine and fellowship" [Acts 2:42]. That is, they *followed* the Apostles (*Parochial and Plain Sermons*, VI, 1842, Sermon 14: "The Fellowship of the Apostles," 1298-1299).

What Catholics believe in faith is that the apostolic doctrine or Christian Tradition (uniquely preserved by the Catholic Church) does not and will not conflict with Holy Scripture. The two are viewed as pieces of a whole, just as Protestants believe in faith that the many parts that make up Holy Scripture do not contradict each other, but form a harmonious, coherent unity. One can believe in faith that an answer to a "difficulty" exists and at the same time not deny that there is (on the surface, anyway) a seeming difficulty that requires much scholarship and study to resolve.

The Bible is central and primary in Catholicism as well, but not *exclusively* authoritative; it is not isolated (Scripture alone), nor can it even logically be so. We maintain that this was the apostolic and patristic viewpoint, and that of Augustine and Aquinas, which we preserve unchanged. We believe in faith and from reason and Scripture, that God will protect the Church from error in its dogmatic pronouncements, because we believe there is one institutional Church and "one faith" (as St. Paul states), handed down from the Apostles.

Protestants believe that God protected Holy Scripture from error, by means of inspiration, even though sinful, fallible men wrote it. Catholics agree with that and also believe that God (the Holy Spirit: John 14-16) can protect His Church from error by means of infallibility (a lesser supernatural gift than inspiration), even though sinful, fallible men are involved in it. If God can do the one thing, he can do the other. Since both are indicated in Scripture and apostolic and patristic tradition, we believe them.

SINNERS IN THE CHURCH

2 Corinthians 11:2-4: "I feel a divine jealousy for you, for I betrothed you to Christ to present you as a pure bride to her one husband. But I am afraid that as the serpent deceived Eve by his cunning, your thoughts will be led astray from a sincere and pure devotion to Christ. For if someone comes and preaches another Jesus than the one we preached, or if you receive a different spirit from the one you received, or if you accept a different gospel from the one you accepted, you submit to it readily enough."

Galatians 1:1-6: "Paul, an apostle — not from men nor through man, but through Jesus Christ and God the Father, who raised him from the dead — and all the brethren who are with me, To the churches of Galatia: Grace to you and peace from God the Father and our Lord Jesus Christ, who gave himself for our sins to deliver us from the present evil age, according to the will of our God and Father; to whom be the glory forever and ever. Amen. I am astonished that you are so quickly deserting him who called you in the grace of Christ and turning to a different gospel."

Revelation 3:1-6: "And to the angel of the church in Sardis write: 'The words of him who has the seven spirits of God and the seven stars. I know your works; you have the name of being alive, and you are dead. Awake, and strengthen what remains and is on the point of death, for I have not found your works perfect in the sight of my God. Remember then what you received and heard; keep that, and repent. If you will not awake, I will come like a thief, and you will not know at what hour I will come upon you. Yet you have still a few names in Sardis, people who have not soiled their garments; and they shall walk with me in white, for they are worthy. He who conquers shall be clad thus in white garments, and I will not blot his name out of the book of life; I will confess his name before my Father and before his angels. He who has an ear, let him hear what the Spirit says to the churches.' "

St. Paul "betrothed" the Corinthians to Christ and writes to the "churches" of Galatia, even though he rebukes both churches for turning to a "different gospel." He does not claim that they never were Christians, nor does he take away that title from them. Jesus refers to the "seven churches" in the book of Revelation, despite the host of sins and shortcomings for which he rebukes them. This is the Catholic position: there are sinners in the Church alongside "saints," as in the parable of the wheat and the tares (Matt. 13:24-30).

Many Protestants persist in believing that the Christian Church can be pure and without sinners or instances of hypocrisy, even though these passages show that this was not anticipated by the Apostles or by our Lord Jesus. In hopes of finding this "pure" church, Protestants proceed to form new sects all the time.

I cite as an example of an advocate of a "pure" church the Mennonite Dietrich Philips, who wrote a treatise entitled *The Church of God*, a portion of his *Enchiridion*, from around the year 1560:

> The fourth ordinance is evangelical separation, without which the congregation of God cannot stand or be maintained. For if the unfruitful branches of the vine are not pruned away, they will injure the good and fruitful branches (John 15:6). If offending members are not cut off, the whole body must perish (Matt. 5:30; 18:7-9); that is, if open sinners, transgressors, and the disorderly are not excluded, the whole congregation must be defiled (1 Cor. 5:13; 1 Thess. 5:14), and if false brethren are retained, we become partakers of their sins. . . .
>
> A little leaven leaveneth the whole lump, and that one scabby sheep contaminates the whole flock (in Williams, 246-247).

A prevalent myth related to this point, that the Protestant "Reformation" was largely concerned with moral rather than doctrinal corruption, must be discarded. It is not even true that early Protestant morality on the whole was on a higher plane than the Catholic morality of the time. Martin Luther and his successor Philip Melanchthon are on record lamenting the state of Protestant morality and neglect of spirituality.

The tendency toward Puritanism in Evangelical Protestantism is, however, contrary to some strong statements by Martin Luther and John Calvin. Luther wrote in 1524:

It is not a fruit of the Spirit to criticize a doctrine by the imperfect life of the teacher. . . . I would have paid little attention to the papists, if only they would teach correctly. Their evil life would not cause much harm (*Letter to the Princes of Saxony Concerning the Rebellious Spirit*, LW, 40, 57).

Likewise, John Calvin recognized that sinners would be in the true Church. He writes very eloquently about it, but this consciousness seems to be lost among many Protestants today, particularly as seen in their criticisms of the Catholic Church:

Our indulgence ought to extend much farther in tolerating imperfection of conduct. . . . For there always have been persons who, imbued with a false persuasion of absolute holiness, as if they had already become a kind of aerial spirits, spurn the society of all in whom they see that something human still remains. Such of old were the Cathari and the Donatists, who were similarly infatuated. Such in the present day are some of the Anabaptists, who would be thought to have made superior progress. . . . Where the Lord requires mercy, they omit it, and give themselves up to immoderate severity. . . . If the Lord declares that the Church will labor under the defect of being burdened with a multitude of wicked until the day of judgment, it is in vain to look for a church altogether free from blemish (Matt. 13).

. . . How, I ask, would those who act so morosely against present churches have acted to the Galatians, who had done all but abandon the gospel (Gal. 1:6), and yet among them the same apostle found churches? (*Institutes*, IV, 1, 13-14).

We see, then, that the opinions of Luther and Calvin — the mainstream Protestant "Reformers" — in this regard, were not appreciably different from the outlook of the Catholic Church. They were concerned about what they felt to be doctrinal, not moral, corruption. They opposed moral corruption as well, but it was not on those grounds that they decided that the Catholic Church was beyond hope of internal reform. The Bible teaches that there are sinners in the true Church.

Chapter Two

Divisions and Denominationalism

CHRISTIANS OUGHT TO BE ONE
AS JESUS AND HIS FATHER ARE ONE

John 17:20-23: " 'I do not pray for these only, but also for those who believe in me through their word, that they may all be one; even as thou, Father, art in me, and I in thee, that they also may be in us, so that the world may believe that thou hast sent me. The glory which thou hast given me I have given to them, that they may be one even as we are one.' "

The Catholic position on Christian unity is fully in accord with biblical texts like this one. We believe that doctrine should be unified and that all Christians should be of one mind and spirit. It is to uphold this biblical injunction that we believe in dogma, hierarchical authority, apostolic Tradition, and a papacy. One may think what he will about all that, but it cannot be denied that Catholicism has traditionally been highly concerned with oneness of doctrine and avoidance of sectarianism and division.

The presence of divisions and denominationalism is one aspect of Protestantism that is widely acknowledged by Protestants themselves (to their credit) as scandalous. Nonetheless, one notices a great reluctance to admit that the existence of such divisions casts any doubt upon the Protestant principles that arguably created this unfortunate state of affairs in the first place.

Protestant apologists use various tactics to avoid the disturbing impact of a passage like John 17:20-23. A debate opponent once suggested to me that Jesus' prayer of unity in John 17 was not the "coerced" dogmatic unity of Catholicism, but rather a "oneness in love." I agreed that unity in love was part of the passage's meaning. But I refused to discount the implication of doctrinal oneness.

Jesus prayed to the Father that the disciples would be "one, even as we are one." And he desires that they (and we) be "completely one" (NRSV). Other translations read "perfect in one" (KJV, NKJV), "perfectly one" (RSV, NEB, REB), in "complete unity" (NIV), and "perfected in unity" (NASB).

It is difficult to maintain that this unity could entail no doctrinal agreement. The Father and the Son do not differ on how one is saved, or on the true nature of the Eucharist or the Church. They would not have disagreements about how the Church is to be governed, or about baptism, or about Arminianism versus Calvinism, or about any number of disputed doctrines over which Protestants endlessly argue among themselves.

They are completely one and in unity in all respects. No one who accepts the Bible as inspired can argue that point. So if we are commanded to have *that* kind of divine unity, it would seem very clear that denominationalism is completely ruled out.

A MULTIPLICITY OF DIVISIONS IS A BAD THING

1 Corinthians 11:18-19: "For, in the first place, when you assemble as a church, I hear that there are divisions among you; and I partly believe it, for there must be factions among you in order that those who are genuine among you may be recognized."

This passage illustrates that St. Paul had the same high concern for oneness and unity in the Body of Christ that our Lord Jesus expressed in our last passage (so that the Catholic emphasis on doctrinal homogeneity is thoroughly biblical).

But Protestants disagree. The same Protestant debate opponent whom I cited in the last example argued that heresy in the modern sense of the word was absolutely foreign to the context of 1 Corinthians 11:18-19. But this opinion was not shared by Protestant Greek scholar Marvin Vincent, who sends the reader to his comment on 2 Peter 2:1, a verse that even my Protestant friend admitted was referring to "dogma":

> A heresy is, strictly, the choice of an opinion contrary to that usually received; thence transferred to the body of those who profess such opinions, and therefore a "sect" . . . commonly in this sense in the NT (Acts 5:17; 15:5; 28:22). . . . See Acts 24:14; 1 Cor. 11:19; Gal. 5:20. The rendering "heretical doctrines" seems to agree better with the context (Vincent, I, 689).

Protestantism is heretical wherever it differs from the "received" opinion of Christian Tradition, according to Vincent and the Bible. Protestantism picked and chose which unbroken apostolic traditions it would continue to uphold and which ones it would jettison. This is precisely the literal meaning of *heresy*.

Again, we find that denominationalism was not at all the intent of the initial founders of Protestantism (although arguably they might have known what their new principles of authority would inevitably produce). John Calvin recognized the absurdity of Protestant divisions and thought that their existence represented an embarrassing disproof of Protestant claims to preeminence over against Catholicism. In a letter to Philip Melanchthon, Luther's successor, dated November 28, 1552 (the issue at hand was a disagreement about free will and limited atonement), he wrote:

[T]he eyes of many are turned upon us, so that the wicked take occasion from our dissensions to speak evil, and the weak are only perplexed by our unintelligible disputations.

And surely it is indicative of a marvelous and monstrous insensibility, that we so readily set at nought that sacred unanimity, by which we ought to be bringing back into the world the angels of heaven. Meanwhile, Satan is busy scattering here and there the seeds of discord, and our folly is made to supply much material (in Bonnet, V, 376-377).

Calvin, in his commentary on 1 Corinthians 1:10 (see the next section) reiterated his viewpoint:

[N]othing is more inconsistent on the part of Christians than to be at variance among themselves, for it is the main article of our religion that we be in harmony among ourselves. . . . It is difficult, indeed, of attainment, but still it is necessary among Christians, from whom there is required not merely one faith, but also one confession.

Protestant denominationalism is, therefore, not only contrary to the clear teaching of Scripture, but also to the noblest intentions of the founders of Protestantism.

PAUL FORBIDS DISSENSIONS AND DENOMINATIONALISM

Romans 16:17: "I appeal to you, brethren, to take note of those who create dissensions and difficulties, in opposition to the doctrine which you have been taught; avoid them."

1 Corinthians 1:10-13: "I appeal to you, brethren, by the name of our Lord Jesus Christ, that all of you agree and that there be no dissensions among you, but that you be united in the same mind and the same judgment. For it has been reported to me by Chloe's people that there is quarreling among you, my brethren. What I mean is that each one of you says, 'I belong to Paul,' or 'I belong to Apollos,' or 'I belong to Cephas,' or 'I belong to Christ.' Is Christ divided? Was Paul crucified for you? Or were you baptized in the name of Paul?"

1 Corinthians 3:3-4: "For you are still of the flesh. For while there is jealousy and strife among you, are you not of the flesh, and behaving like ordinary men? For when one says, 'I belong to Paul,' and another, 'I belong to Apollos,' are you not merely men?

1 Corinthians 12:25: ". . . that there may be no discord in the body, but that the members may have the same care for one another."

Philippians 2:2: "Complete my joy by being of the same mind, having the same love, being in full accord and of one mind."

Again, we see the very strong biblical and Pauline emphasis on Christian doctrinal unity, yet the Catholic Church is criticized for teaching the same thing (and, naturally, locating the focus for this unity within its own Tradition). It is extremely difficult to rationalize away all of these passages and act as if they did not deal a crushing blow to Protestantism, insofar as it is clearly divided and hopelessly multiplying into further sects.

In my opinion, this is one of the most compelling and unanswerable disproofs of Protestantism as a system to be found in the Bible. But Protestants have no choice. They feel that Protestantism must be bolstered up as an alternative to Catholicism, no matter how many serious contradictions with Scripture exist within it. So they continue to try to explain away these Bible passages.

This is why the Catholic Magisterium, apostolic succession, the papacy, binding ecumenical councils, and the notion of an unbroken, continuous apostolic Tradition preserved uniquely by the Holy Spirit in an actual concrete institution are necessary.

As a remarkable example of this losing, futile battle with Scripture in the area of doctrinal and ecclesiastical oneness, I submit the argument of a Calvinist apologist whom I engaged in a "live chat" debate one night on the Internet. I first asked him, "On what basis — by what criterion — does a person discover truth within the Protestant system, seeing that all parties in that system appeal to the Bible, yet cannot agree on a host of issues?"

In particular, I wondered, why I should believe his view of baptism (Presbyterian: infant, non-regenerative), over against that of Martin Luther (infant, regenerative) and the Baptist position (adult, non-regenerative)?

He said that one should not "consult people but the Bible." He later fleshed out a second response: the Bible teaches that disagreements are to be expected, thus they pose no difficulty for the doctrinal disunity within Protestantism.

My Protestant friend cited Romans 14 in support of his contention that doctrinal diversity on so-called "secondary issues" was permissible, according to the Bible. I knew a little bit about what was in Romans 14, so I asked him to tell me what particular doctrines were discussed in that chapter which would allow him to conclude that doctrinal division was acceptable.

He cited only the disagreement over the Sabbath, or the day of worship. I replied that this was irrelevant to our discussion, since Protestants and Catholics agree on a Sunday Sabbath, and that pretty much the only dissenters are Seventh-Day Adventists. He could give me no other doctrine discussed in Romans 14, although he continued to refer to the chapter as a justification for Protestantism's relativism-in-practice in many doctrines (what he described as allowable and fully expected "diversity").

There is a good reason why no more examples from Romans 14 were given: the chapter deals only with quite "undoctrinal" matters, such as what we should eat or not eat (14:2-3, 14-17), and esteeming one day above another (14:5). That is *all* that is there!

Yet this professional Calvinist apologist appealed to this passage in defense of his notion that doctrinal issues such as baptism and the Eucharist are entirely matters of individual discretion, admitting of diverse viewpoints, and that no one should be troubled by the fact that Protestants cannot agree among themselves. This is not only a weak biblical argument; it is expressly *contrary* to the passages above.

The exceedingly serious problem of denominationalism exists in Protestantism and always will, for it cannot be overcome by any Protestant internal principles, no matter how nuanced or sophisticated or in line with "Reformation heritage." Protestantism cannot settle its internal differences; each branch or sect can only (ultimately arbitrarily) assert its own authority.

Thus, Calvin asserts his own authority, Luther his, Zwingli and Menno Simons (Mennonites) and George Fox (Quakers) and William Booth (Salvation Army) theirs. Many independent Protestants today claim to be subject to no human leaders or traditions, yet inevitably follow their own traditions. Protestants have no way of resolving these "denominational dichotomies." They will continue to split, and each party or faction will justify its split based on appeals to the one Bible.

To put it in very practical terms: how does the man on the street, who has to choose between competing factions, determine truth under Protestant assumptions? He has to choose whether Calvin or Luther is right and then go on to choose among the competing Lutheran or Calvinist camps. Why should Calvin have any more authority than Luther had? Each simply claimed it for himself (as anointed from on high) and demanded allegiance.

In the final analysis, the Protestant is forced to appeal to one of two equally insufficient and unsatisfactory solutions:

A. Claim that his own brand of Protestantism is the true one to be believed above all others. This was, of course, the standard approach taken by virtually all the early Protestant factions (thus they rather comically and ironically anathematized and damned each other).

B. Pretend that doctrines on which Protestants disagree (almost always doctrines other than those on which they agree even with Catholics and Orthodox) are "secondary" and not important enough to fight over. I often describe this as a *de facto* doctrinal relativism, and it is the usual course taken today.

John Calvin tried to take a somewhat intermediate position. He recognized the distinction between doctrines of lesser and greater importance (that is, the position B above, which is the usual Protestant argument today in justifying denominationalism):

For all the heads of true doctrine are not in the same position. Some are so necessary to be known that all must hold them to be fixed and undoubted as the proper essentials of religion: for instance, that God is one, that Christ is God and the Son of God, that our salvation depends on the mercy of God, and the like. Others, again, which are the subject of controversy among the churches, do not destroy the unity of the faith (*Institutes*, IV, 1, 12).

On the other hand, he did not countenance separation and further division based on disputes over these secondary doctrines:

The words of the Apostle are, "Let us therefore, as many as be perfect, be thus minded; and if in anything ye be otherwise minded, God shall reveal even this unto you" (Phil.

3:15). Does he not sufficiently intimate that a difference of opinion as to these matters which are not absolutely necessary, ought not to be a ground of dissension among Christians? (*Institutes*, IV, 1, 12).

"Solutions" A and B are equally unbiblical, unhistorical, and illogical. Calvin's position is also ultimately incoherent and clashes with his doctrine of the invisible Church (examined earlier). The problems cannot be resolved. Catholics can at least offer internally coherent and consistent answers and solutions to these vexing problems of authority, whereas the Protestant system always inevitably breaks down at some point.

Chapter Three

Bible and Tradition

THE NECESSITY OF
AUTHORITATIVE INTERPRETATION

Nehemiah 8:8: "And they read from the book, from the law of God, clearly; and they gave the sense, so that the people understood the reading" (cf. Mark 4:33-34).

Acts 8:27-31: "And he rose and went. And behold, an Ethiopian, a eunuch, a minister of the Candace, queen of the Ethiopians, in charge of all her treasure, had come to Jerusalem to worship and was returning; seated in his chariot, he was reading the prophet Isaiah. And the Spirit said to Philip, 'Go up and join this chariot.' So Philip ran to him, and heard him reading Isaiah the prophet, and asked, 'Do you understand what you are reading?' And he said, 'How can I, unless someone guides me?' And he invited Philip to come up and sit with him."

2 Peter 1:20: "First of all, you must understand this, that no prophecy of scripture is a matter of one's own interpretation" (cf. 2 Pet. 3:15-16).

Catholics hold that Scripture is a fairly clear document and able to be understood by the average reader, but also that the Church is needed to provide a doctrinal norm, an overall framework for determining proper biblical interpretation. Both Luther and Calvin underemphasize the guidance of the Church in understanding the Bible and assert the perspicuity, or clearness, and the self-interpreting nature of Scripture, in terms of its overall teaching. Luther wrote:

> [T]he contents of Scripture are as clear as can be. . . . If words are obscure in one place, they are clear in another. . . . To many people a great deal remains obscure; but that is due, not to any lack of clarity in Scripture, but to their own blindness and dullness (*The Bondage of the Will*, II: "Review of Erasmus' Preface"; ii: "Of the perspicuity of Scripture"; from Packer, 71-72).

The scriptural passages just cited would seem to contradict Luther's notion (although Catholics would agree with him that the blindness of men causes many of the diverse interpretations — precisely why an authority beyond the Bible itself is needed). The teaching authority of the Church and its necessity to preserve true doctrine and to prevent dissensions and heresies has always been a major issue between Catholics and Protestants.

Does the Bible itself teach that it can always be understood by anyone who is filled with the Holy Spirit, as Luther claims (elsewhere he claimed, famously, that even a "plowboy" could understand it)? This is not the outlook of the writers of the Old Testament. Indications are numerous:

Moses was told to *teach* the Hebrews the statutes and the decisions, not just *read* them to the people (Exod. 18:20). The Levitical priests interpreted the biblical injunctions (Deut. 17:11). The penalty for disobedience was death (Deut. 17:12, 33:10; cf. 19:16-17; 2 Chron. 15:3, 19:8-10; Mal. 2:6-8). Ezra, a priest and a scribe, taught the Jewish Law to Israel, and his authority was binding, under pain of imprisonment, banishment, loss of goods, and even death (Ezra 7:6, 10, 25-26).

In Nehemiah 8:1-8, Ezra reads the Law of Moses to the people in Jerusalem (8:3). In 8:7 we find thirteen Levites who assisted Ezra and *who helped the people to understand the Law.* Much earlier, in King Jehoshaphat's reign, we find Levites exercising the same function (2 Chron. 17:8-9). There is no *sola Scriptura* with its associated idea of perspicuity here.

The two passages above from the New Testament demonstrate that this principle did not change with the New Covenant. The Apostles promulgated an authoritative tradition (see the next section), and they did not tolerate dissension from it (see the previous chapter on divisions and denominationalism). Once again, we find that an important Protestant distinctive is not biblical. So how do they attempt to explain this discrepancy? John Calvin, in his *Commentaries*, makes the following argument, pertaining to 1 Peter 1:20:

> But the Papists are doubly foolish, when they conclude from this passage that no interpretation of a private man ought to be deemed authoritative. For they pervert what Peter says, that they may claim for their own councils the chief right of interpreting Scripture; but in this they act indeed childishly; for Peter calls interpretation *private*, not that of every individual, in order to prohibit each one to interpret; but he shews that whatever men bring of their own is profane. . . . The faithful, inwardly illuminated by the Holy Spirit, acknowledge nothing but what God says in his word.

I would like to apply Calvin's principle and reasoning and demonstrate that it ultimately reduces to absurdity and the utmost impracticality. Calvin, like Luther, despised the sectarianism that proliferated as a result of Protestant principles of authority, such as private judgment and the perspicuity of Scripture.

But neither Calvin nor Luther seemed to see the obvious causal connection between their new principles and the proliferation of Protestant sects. Luther claimed authority to overthrow a host of traditions that had been held for 1,500 years. On what basis did he do so? To probe that issue and get to the bottom of it, one might construct a hypothetical dialogue between Luther and a Catholic critic that would run something like this:

Luther (L): The Catholic Church is incorrect in beliefs a, b, c, and d.

Catholic (C): Why do you say that?

L: Because what you teach is unbiblical.

C: What gives you the authority to determine such a thing?

L: My authority is the Word of God, to which my conscience is captive.

C: We grant your sincerity, but not everyone agrees with your interpretation of Holy Scripture. Why should we believe you over against Church Tradition?

L: Because God has appointed me as the restorer of the gospel.

C: How do you know that? Why should we believe it?

L: God's Word will make it manifest.

C: But what happens when your fellow Protestants, such as Calvin, Zwingli, and the Anabaptists, disagree with you?

L: One must determine which view is more biblical.

C: How does one go about that, since your movement has no one leader, but rather, increasing numbers of sects who oppose each other on one or more grounds?

L: From now on, I shall no longer do you the honor of allowing you, or even an angel from heaven, to judge my teaching or to examine it. Instead, I shall let myself be heard and, as St. Peter teaches, give an explanation and defense of my teaching to all the world — 1 Peter 3:15. I shall not have it judged by any man, not even by any angel. For since I am certain of it, I shall be your judge and even the angels' judge through this teaching, as St. Paul say — 1 Cor. 6:3 — so that whoever does not accept my teaching may not be saved — for it is God's and not mine. Therefore, my judgment is also not mine but God's.[2]

C: But don't you see that when Calvin or Zwingli disagree with you, they do so on the same grounds you claim for yourself, and that no one can figure out who is telling the truth unless there is a "court of final appeal"?

L: My truth is plain in the Bible.

C: That's what Zwingli says, too.

L: He is damned and out of the Church because he denies what has always been taught by the Church: that the body and blood of Jesus are truly present after consecration. It pains me that Zwingli and his followers take offense at my saying that "what I write must be true." Zwingli, Karlstadt, and the other heretics have in-deviled, through-deviled, over-deviled, corrupt hearts and lying mouths.

C: The truth is that which has always been held by the Church, just as you yourself argued with regard to the Real Presence in the Eucharist. Why, then, do you deny other Catholic doctrines that have an equally long history?

L: Because they are unbiblical.

C: According to whom?

L: According to the Bible.

C: As interpreted by you?

L: Yes, because, as I said already, whoever does not accept my teaching may not be saved, for it is God's and not mine. Do we not

---

[2] Actual words of Luther: *Against the Spiritual Estate of the Pope and the Bishops Falsely So-Called*, July 1522; LW, 39, 239-299; quote from 248-249.

read in the Old Testament that God commonly raised up only one prophet at a time? I say not that I am a prophet, but I do say that the more you despise me and esteem yourselves, the more reason you have to fear that I may be a prophet. If I am not a prophet, yet for my own self I am certain that the Word of God is with me and not with you, for I have the Scriptures on my side, and you have only your own doctrine.[3]

C: So we either accept your authority and word as the preeminent Bible expositor and deliverer of Christian truth of all time, and possibly a prophet, or so much the worse for us?

L: Yes, because God would have it so. You are obviously wrong, and I must be right, because my teaching lines up with Scripture. You disagree with me not because of any lack of clarity in Scripture, but because of your own blindness and dullness.

And so on and so forth. It goes on and on like this, but the underlying assumptions of Luther are never *proven*; they are merely *assumed*. If a pope dared to proclaim such an unspeakably outrageous thing, Protestants would not accept it in a million years. But when *Luther* does it, it is accepted with blind faith that he is right and the Catholics are wrong, because "everyone knows" that Protestants are the "Bible people" and Catholics are not! Catholics follow crusty, dead traditions of men who were condemned by Jesus and are like the Pharisees, et cetera, et cetera.

That is what it always falls back on, because appeals to the Bible inescapably reduce to disputes over whose *interpretation* is correct. This is the circular nature of competing Protestant theologies. There is no way to choose between Calvin and Luther, except arbitrariness, irrational faith, or appeal to one's own judgment.

---

[3] Closely based on actual words from Luther's tract *An Argument in Defense of All the Articles of Martin Luther Wrongly Condemned in the Roman Bull*, 1521, in Jacobs, III, 13-14.

Calvin has no more authority than Luther did. They both simply proclaimed it, and people followed them. At the same time, they railed against the Catholic exercise of authority, which was self-consistent, and far easier to trace back through history, in an unbroken apostolic succession (precisely as the Church Fathers argued for their authority in proclaiming true doctrine over against heresy).

This was the inner logic and dynamic of Luther's new perspective, set forth at the Diet of Worms in 1521 (the famous confrontation where he cried, "Here I stand!"). Yet few Protestants will admit that it is unreasonable or a circular argument, and far more objectionable and implausible than the Catholic stance in reaction to Luther. It sounds wonderful and noble and almost self-evidently true to choose (as Luther did at Worms) the "Bible and plain reason" rather than the "traditions of men." But of course that is a false dilemma and caricature of Luther's choice from the get-go.

It is a vicious logical circle for Protestants, any way one looks at it. This is what happens when "private interpretation" is championed, contrary to 2 Peter 1:20. It was already an unbiblical concept even before its fruit in history became evident.

THE BINDING AUTHORITY OF
TRADITION, ACCORDING TO ST. PAUL

1 Corinthians 11:2: "I commend you because you remember me in everything and maintain the traditions even as I have delivered them to you."

1 Thessalonians 2:13: "And we also thank God constantly for this, that when you received the word of God which you heard from us, you accepted it not as the word of men but as what it really is, the word of God, which is at work in you believers."

> **2 Thessalonians 2:15:** "So then, brethren, stand firm and hold to the traditions which you were taught by us, either by word of mouth or by letter."

> **2 Thessalonians 3:6:** "Now we command you, brethren, in the name of our Lord Jesus Christ, that you keep away from any brother who is living in idleness and not in accord with the tradition that you received from us."

Catholics believe that there is such a thing as a binding, authoritative Sacred Tradition and that it is explicitly indicated in the Bible (notably in the above passages). We believe that the Church is the guardian of this apostolic Tradition, passed down continuously through history from the Apostles.

With regard to Tradition, the question is not *whether* but *which?* Protestants have traditions just as Catholics do. But they are less grounded in history. They are arbitrary (excepting those that agree with the Catholic Church, because they can be traced back historically). Since Luther was starting a new tradition, he could not appeal to history and thus was forced (rather than admit he was actually wrong about anything) to rely on the Bible alone. Yet the Bible itself points to an authoritative Church and Tradition.

St. Thomas More expresses the Catholic perspective on apostolic Christian Tradition in a tract, *Response to Luther*, in 1523, where he comments on 2 Thessalonians 2:15:

> The preservation of both word and letter is equally charged by the Apostle. Extrascriptural matter was thus handed down, and on a binding, not a take-it-or-leave-it basis! What do you say to that, Luther?
>
> [Y]ou continue dully to insist upon the written as the only valid form of transmission, and doggedly persist in ignoring the scriptural evidence (in Dolan, 115, 117).

John Calvin comments on 1 Corinthians 11:2 as follows, offering no argument whatsoever, but merely resorting to the *ad hominem* (or should we say *ad ecclesiam?*) fallacy:

> Papists . . . arm themselves with this passage for the purpose of defending their traditions . . . [which] include not merely certain foolish superstitions, and puerile ceremonies, with which they are stuffed, but also all kinds of gross abomination, directly contrary to the plain word of God, and their tyrannical laws, which are mere torments to men's consciences. In this way there is nothing that is so foolish, nothing so absurd — in fine, nothing so monstrous, as not to have shelter under this pretext, and to be painted over with this varnish.

This is a superb example of how even the best and most influential Protestant exegetes deal improperly with Holy Scripture when it teaches something contrary to their theological system.

> I do not deny that there were certain traditions of the Apostles that were not committed to writing, but I do not admit that they were parts of doctrine or related to things necessary for salvation.

Here, Calvin moves on from the silly attacks and name-calling, but his argument continues to be based on thin evidence. Certainly the biblical text under consideration contains no information to support Calvin's position. Rather it derives from Calvin's own opinion, simply because it fits into his system. It is entirely arbitrary. When Paul refers to tradition, he makes no indication that it has to do only with "things necessary for salvation."

In his commentary on the similar verse, 2 Thessalonians 2:15, Calvin (in the surrounding context) at least acknowledges a wider scope of tradition, but refuses to give any quarter to the Catholic Church:

> Papists . . . act a still more ridiculous part in making it their
> aim to pass off, under this, the abominable sink of their own
> superstitions, as though they were the traditions of Paul. . . .
> Now, what do these Epistles contain but pure doctrine,
> which overturns to the very foundation the whole of the
> Papacy, and every invention that is at variance with the
> simplicity of the Gospel?

In the theologically supercharged sixteenth century, it was probably impossible for the polemics to have been otherwise, but it is disappointing that a man of the intellect of John Calvin could not discuss the larger issues of Tradition, Church, and authority without resorting to anti-Catholic mudslinging. Be that as it may, it is scarcely possible to discuss that issue constructively, because (in my opinion) Protestants are so afraid that any serious discussion of Tradition will cast doubt on *sola Scriptura* and lead to undesired "Catholic" consequences.

As an example of the typical, nonconstructive dialogue between Catholics and Protestants even today, the following is a stripped-down, paraphrased version of a discourse I had with an anti-Catholic Reformed apologist. Note how my opponent made a claim but never backed it up with any specificity. It just hung in midair. But he did not seem to recognize that this would pose any problem for his position.

P: Protestants, too, firmly accept what the Apostles taught. Indeed, maintaining the original, apostolic message is a powerful argument against the corrupt innovations and unbiblical additions of Rome over time.

C: Why not boldly tell us, then, precisely what the Apostles taught? In particular, in those areas where Protestants don't agree with each other. In order to have fidelity to an apostolic message, one must define what it *is*.

P: That's easily answered, Dave. We have the New Testament, which is filled with the Apostles' teaching. One such teaching is that we are justified by faith, giving us peace with God: Romans 5:1. The Apostles also taught that Jesus Christ was God: Colossians 2:9. Do you wish to contend that the Bible cannot answer these questions?

C: It's ultimately irrelevant what I think, because I'm asking you. Please tell me what it teaches on these issues.

P: Those who go by the title "Protestant" disagree on all the points above [I had listed eighteen]; so do Roman Catholics. So what? Does that mean, then, that the Bible is insufficient?

C: Are you going to maintain seriously that the Apostles, in the Bible, did not address issues on my list such as: baptism, the Eucharist, church government, regeneration, sanctification, Tradition, or the spiritual gifts? I'm astonished. Why don't you, then, select just five?

P: So you are arguing that a Christian believer with a Bible cannot find out what the apostolic message was unless Roman "tradition" informs him?

C: According to your logic, one can know what the message is, without the Catholic Church, but they can't tell *someone else* what it *is*, what it *consists* of!

P: I think, Dave, that you are fully aware that your question has been and will be answered.

C: I'm eagerly awaiting your response — nothing fancy, just a laundry list of the true apostolic teachings. At least Luther and Calvin had the strength of their convictions to excommunicate other Protestants for dissidence, because they truly believed in their own brand of Christianity. There is something to be said for that.

P: I refuse to anathematize a brother in Christ for incorrect beliefs on baptism or Holy Communion. But I will certainly point out his error. What you don't seem to understand is that unity of belief is worthless if that belief is a falsehood!

C: I agree one hundred percent. Thus, the question boils down to, as always: Is what the Catholic Church teaches true or false? And the same for Protestantism.

P: You know what the biblical position is on these [eighteen] topics.

C: This is the whole point! We know, but you can't figure it out. Hence your reluctance to answer. I can think of no better reason. A short answer to my question surely wouldn't put you out.

P: But you don't accept what the Bible teaches.

C: I supposedly don't accept what the Bible teaches on these points, but you don't have the courtesy to explain to me just what it *is* that it teaches on them.

P: Instead of the Bible, you accept a Catholic authority that tells you differently.

C: Different from what? Again, if I don't have your answer, what do you expect me to believe? If this isn't *The Emperor's New Clothes*, I don't know what is.

P: Tell me again, Dave: do you claim that the Bible is insufficient to resolve these matters? That we can't learn what the Bible's position on tradition is, for instance? That a serious exegesis of texts can't give us any knowledge?

C: No, no, no. Now, how about your equally forthright answer to me?

P: All Christians have traditions of some sort. But they are fallible outside of Scripture. We ought to test all our traditions by Scripture.

C: Yes, but since you Protestants can't agree with the *interpretation* of Scripture, of what practical use is an infallible Bible? If the interpretation is fallible and contradictory, then, practically speaking, the Bible in effect is no more infallible than its differing interpretations.

P: Christian unity does not exist. Each person must remain true to the Word of God.

C: Theological certainty does not exist? So Christianity is reduced to philosophy. That is a slap in God's face (although I'm sure you don't mean it in that way). The God I serve is able, through His Holy Spirit, to impart truth to us, as the Bible teaches. "True to the Word"? You seek to be; so do I. Now what do we do? True to the Word, yet so many disagreements over that very Word of truth. How do we resolve this dilemma? Throw up our hands in despair? Or admit that Catholics might be on to something?

ORAL AND EXTRABIBLICAL
TRADITION IN THE NEW TESTAMENT

> **Matthew 2:23:** "And he went and dwelt in a city called Nazareth, that what was spoken by the prophets might be fulfilled, 'He shall be called a Nazarene.' "

> **Matthew 23:1-3:** "Then said Jesus to the crowds and to his disciples, 'The scribes and the Pharisees sit on Moses' seat; so practice and observe whatever they tell you, but not what they do; for they preach, but do not practice.' "

Catholics believe that the tradition found in the Bible also includes an oral component. The reference in Matthew 2:23 — "He shall be called a Nazarene" — cannot be found in the Old Testament, yet it was passed down by the prophets. Thus, a prophecy, which is considered to be God's Word was passed down orally, rather than through Scripture.

Likewise, Matthew 23:2-3: Jesus teaches that the scribes and Pharisees have a legitimate, binding authority, based on *Moses' seat*, which phrase (or idea) cannot be found anywhere in the Old Testament. It is found in the (originally oral) Mishna, where a sort of teaching succession from Moses on down is taught. Thus, apostolic succession, whereby the Catholic Church, in its priests and

bishops and popes, claims to be merely the custodian of an inherited apostolic Tradition, is also prefigured by Jewish oral tradition,
as approved (at least partially) by Jesus himself.

Other examples of extrabiblical and oral tradition acknowledged by the New Testament writers include:

• 1 Corinthians 10:4, where St. Paul refers to a rock
which "followed" the Jews through the Sinai wilderness.
The Old Testament says nothing about such miraculous
movement, in the related passages about Moses striking the
rock to produce water (Exod. 17:1-7; Num. 20:2-13). Rab-
binic tradition, however, does.

• 1 Peter 3:19, where St. Peter describes Christ's journey to Sheol/Hades ("he went and preached to the spirits
in prison"), draws directly from the Jewish apocalyptic book
1 Enoch (12-16). Jude 14-15 directly quotes from 1 Enoch
1:9 and even states that Enoch prophesied.

• Jude 9, which concerns a dispute between Michael the
archangel and Satan over Moses' body, cannot be paralleled
in the Old Testament, and appears to be a recounting of an
oral Jewish tradition.

• In 2 Timothy 3:8, the reference to Jannes and Jambres
cannot be found in the related Old Testament passage
(Exod. 7:8 ff.).

• James 5:17 mentions a lack of rain for three years,
which is likewise absent from the relevant Old Testament
passage in 1 Kings 17.

Since Jesus and the Apostles acknowledge authoritative Jewish oral tradition (in so doing, raising some of it literally to the
level of written revelation), we are hardly at liberty to assert that
it is altogether illegitimate. Jesus attacked corrupt traditions
only, not tradition per se, and not all oral tradition. According to a

strict sola Scriptura viewpoint, this would be inadmissible, it seems to me.

Jesus clearly distinguishes what is called the *tradition of the elders* (Mark 7:3, 5) from the legitimate Tradition, by saying, "You leave the commandment of God, and hold fast the tradition of men" (Mark 7:8; cf. 7:9).

How do Protestants deal with these "anomalous" facts? Presbyterian commentator Albert Barnes, in his famous *Notes*, resorted to what might be deemed special pleading, to evade the consequences of an authoritative nonbiblical tradition, in his comment on Matthew 2:23:

> The words here are not found in any of the books of the Old Testament; and there has been much difficulty in ascertaining the meaning of this passage. . . . The character of the people of Nazareth was such that they were proverbially despised and condemned: John 1:46; 7:52. To come from Nazareth, therefore, or *to be a Nazarene*, was the same as to be despised, and esteemed of low birth; *to be a root out of dry ground, having no form or comeliness.* . . . When Matthew says, therefore, that the prophecies were fulfilled, it means *that the predictions of the prophets that he should be of humble life, and rejected, were fully accomplished in his being an inhabitant of Nazareth, and despised as such.*

Needless to say, with this sort of exegesis, involving a wholly arbitrary personal decision as to what the writer was referring to, rather than texts themselves, almost anything can be proven. But at least Barnes gives it the old college try, and we must admire his ingenuity. Jamieson, Fausset, and Brown are equally speculative in their commentary on this passage:

> The best explanation of the origin of this name appears to be that which traces it to the word *netzer* in Isaiah 11:1 — the

small *twig, sprout,* or sucker, which the prophet there says, "shall come forth from the stem (or rather, 'stump') of Jesse, the branch which should fructify from his roots." The little town of Nazareth, mentioned neither in the Old Testament nor in Josephus, was probably so called from its insignificance: a weak twig in contrast to a stately tree.

Reformed Baptist apologist and expert on *sola Scriptura* James White offered a two-page response to the Catholic apologetic use of Matthew 23:1-3 and Moses' seat. I shall quote the heart of his subtle but thoroughly fallacious argument:

> Some Roman Catholics present this passage as proof that a source of extrabiblical authority received the blessing of the Lord Jesus. It has been alleged that the concept of "Moses' seat" is in fact a refutation of *sola Scriptura*, for not only is this concept not found in the Old Testament, but Jesus seemingly gives His approbation to this extrascriptural tradition. . . .
>
> The "Moses' seat" refers to a seat in the front of the synagogue on which the teacher of the Law sat while reading from the Scriptures. Synagogue worship, of course, came into being long after Moses' day, so those who attempt to make this an oral tradition going back to Moses are engaging in wishful thinking (White, 100).

White agrees that the notion is not found in the Old Testament, but maintains that it cannot be traced back to Moses. Yet the Catholic argument here does not rest on whether it can be traced historically to Moses, but on the fact that it is not found in the Old Testament. Thus, White concedes a fundamental point of the Catholic argument concerning authority and *sola Scriptura.*

White then cites Protestant Bible scholar Robert Gundry in agreement, to the effect that Jesus was binding Christians to the

Pharisaical law, but not "their interpretative traditions." This passage concerned only "the law itself" with the "antinomians" in mind. How Gundry arrives at such a conclusion remains to be seen. White's query about the Catholic interpretation, "Is this sound exegesis?" can just as easily be applied to Gundry's fine-tuned distinctions that help him avoid any implication of a binding extrabiblical tradition. White continues:

> There was nothing in the tradition of having someone read from the Scriptures while sitting on Moses' seat that was in conflict with the Scriptures. . . . It is quite proper to listen and obey the words of the one who reads from the Law or the Prophets, for one is not hearing a man speaking in such a situation, but is listening to the very words of God (White, 101).

This is true as far as it goes, but it is essentially a *non sequitur* and amounts to a "reading into," or eisegesis of the passage (which is ironic, because now *White* plays the role of "a man speaking" and distorting "the very words of God"). Jesus said, "'The scribes and the Pharisees sit on Moses' seat; so practice and observe whatever they tell you, but not what they do; for they preach, but do not practice.'"

First, it should be noted that nowhere in the actual text is the notion that the Pharisees are *only* reading the Old Testament Scripture when sitting on Moses' seat. It is an assumption gratuitously smuggled in from a presupposed position of *sola Scriptura*.

Secondly, White's assumption that Jesus is referring literally to Pharisees sitting on a seat in the synagogue and reading (the Old Testament only) — and that alone — is more forced and woodenly literalistic than the far more plausible interpretation that this was simply a term denoting received authority.

It reminds one of the old silly Protestant tale that the popes speak infallibly and *ex cathedra* (*cathedra* is the Greek word for *seat* in Matthew 23:2) only when sitting in a certain chair in the Vatican — because the phrase means literally "from the bishop's chair" — whereas it was a *figurative* and idiomatic usage).

Jesus says that they sat "on Moses' seat; so practice and observe whatever they tell you." In other words, because they had the authority, based on the position of occupying Moses' seat, they were to be obeyed. It is like referring to a chairman of a company or committee. He occupies the "chair"; therefore he has authority. No one thinks he has the authority only when he sits in a certain chair reading the corporation charter or the Constitution or some other official document.

Yet this is how White would exclusively interpret Jesus' words. *The Eerdmans Bible Dictionary* (a widely used Protestant reference source), in its article, "Seat," allows White's reading as a secondary interpretation, but seems to regard the primary meaning of this term in the manner I have described:

> References to seating in the Bible are almost all to such as a representation of honor and authority. . . .
>
> According to Jesus, the scribes and Pharisees occupy "Moses' seat" (Matt. 23:2), having the authority and ability to interpret the law of Moses correctly; here "seat" is both a metaphor for judicial authority and also a reference to a literal stone seat in the front of many synagogues that would be occupied by an authoritative teacher of the law (Myers, 919-920).

The *International Standard Bible Encyclopedia* (another standard source), in its article "Seat," takes the same position, commenting specifically on our verse:

> It is used also of the exalted position occupied by men of marked rank or influence, either in good or evil (Matt. 23:2; Ps. 1:1) (Orr, IV, 2710).

White makes no mention of these considerations, but it is difficult to believe that he is not aware of them (since he is a Bible scholar well acquainted with the nuances of biblical meanings). They do not fit in very well with the case he is trying to make, so he omits them. But the reader is thereby left with an incomplete picture.

Thirdly, because they had the authority and no indication is given that Jesus thought they had it only when simply reading Scripture, it would follow that Christians were, therefore, bound to elements of Pharisaical teaching that were not only nonscriptural, but based on oral tradition, for this is what Pharisees believed. They fully accepted the binding authority of oral tradition (the Sadducees were the ones who were the Jewish *sola Scripturists* and liberals of the time). The reputable Protestant source *The New Bible Dictionary* describes their beliefs in this respect, in its article "Pharisees":

> [T]he Torah was not merely "law" but also "instruction," i.e., it consisted not merely of fixed commandments but was adaptable to changing conditions. . . . This adaptation or inference was the task of those who had made a special study of the Torah, and a majority decision was binding on all. . . .
>
> The commandments were further applied by analogy to situations not directly covered by the Torah. All these developments together with thirty-one customs of "immemorial usage" formed the "oral law" . . . the full development of which is later than the New Testament. Being convinced that they had the right interpretation of the Torah, they claimed that these "traditions of the elders" (Mark 7:3) came from Moses on Sinai (Douglas, 981-982).

Likewise, *The Oxford Dictionary of the Christian Church* notes in its article on the Pharisees:

Unlike the Sadducees, who tried to apply Mosaic Law precisely as it was given, the Pharisees allowed some interpretation of it to make it more applicable to different situations, and they regarded these oral interpretations as of the same level of importance as the Law itself (Cross, 1077).

Fourthly, it was precisely the extrabiblical (especially apocalyptic) elements of Pharisaical Judaism that New Testament Christianity adopted and developed for its own — doctrines such as resurrection, the soul, the afterlife, eternal reward or damnation, and angelology and demonology (all of which the Sadducees rejected). The Old Testament had relatively little to say about these things, and what it did assert was in a primitive, kernel form. But the postbiblical literature of the Jews (led by the mainstream Pharisaical tradition) had plenty to say about them. Therefore, this was another instance of Christianity utilizing nonbiblical literature and traditions in its own doctrinal development.

Fifthly, Paul shows the high priest Ananias respect, even when the latter strikes him on the mouth and does not deal with matters strictly of the Old Testament and the Law, but with the question of whether Paul was teaching wrongly and should be stopped (Acts 23:1-5). A few verses later, Paul states, "I am a Pharisee, a son of Pharisees" (23:6), and it is noted that the Pharisees and Sadducees in the assembly were divided and that the Sadducees "say that there is no resurrection, nor angel, nor spirit; but the Pharisees acknowledge them all" (23:7-8). Some Pharisees defended Paul (23:9).

Next, White mentions — presumably as a parallel to the Pharisees and Moses' seat — Nehemiah 8, a passage that I dealt with previously:

Indeed, when Ezra read the Law to the people in Nehemiah, chapter 8, the people listened attentively and cried "Amen! Amen!" at the hearing of God's Word (White, 101).

He conveniently neglects to mention, however, that Ezra's Levite assistants, as recorded in the next two verses after the Evangelical-sounding *Amens*, "helped the people to *understand* the law" (8:7) and "gave the sense, so that the people *understood* the reading" (8:8).

So this supposedly analogous example (that is, if presented in its *entirety*; not selectively for polemical purposes) does not support the position of White and Gundry that the authority of the Pharisees applied only insofar as they sat and *read* the Old Testament to the people (functioning as a sort of ancient collective Alexander Scourby, reading the Bible onto a cassette tape for mass consumption), not when they also *interpreted* (which was part and parcel of the Pharisaical outlook and approach).

One does not find in the Old Testament individual Hebrews questioning teaching authority. *Sola Scriptura* simply is not there. No matter how hard White and other Protestants try to read it into the Old Testament, it cannot be done. Nor can it be read into the New Testament. White, however, writes:

> And who can forget the result of Josiah's discovery of the Book of the Covenant in 2 Chronicles 34? (White, 101).

Indeed, this was a momentous occasion. But if the implication is that the Law was self-evident simply upon being *read*, per *sola Scriptura*, this is untrue to the Old Testament, for, again, we are informed in the same book that priests and Levites "taught in Judah, having the book of the law of the Lord with them; they went about through all the cities of Judah and taught among the people" (2 Chron. 17:9), and that the Levites "taught all Israel" (2 Chron. 35:3). They did not just read; they *taught*, and that involved interpretation. And the people had no right of private judgment, to dissent from what was taught.

White and all Protestants believe that any individual Christian has the right and duty to rebuke their pastors if what they are teaching is "unbiblical" (that is, according to the lone individual). This is an elegant, quaint theory indeed, on paper, but it does not quite work the same way in practice. I know this from my own experience as a former Protestant, for when I rebuked my Assemblies of God pastor in a private letter (because he had preached from the pulpit, "Keep your pastors honest"), I was publicly renounced and rebuked from the pulpit (in a most paranoid, alarmist manner) as a theologically inexperienced rabble-rouser trying to cause division.

Kim Riddlebarger, an expert in historical theology, in dealing with the same passage, assumes what he is trying to prove (what is known in logic as begging the question or a circular argument):

> The biblical case for *sola Scriptura* becomes even stronger when one looks to the words of our Lord on the subject. . . . Jesus instructs us to obey the Old Testament (Matt. 23:3). . . . Is the Old Testament incomplete in this regard, requiring a "sacred" tradition to complement it? On the contrary, Jesus declares that the Old Testament alone is authoritative in matters of doctrine. . . . There is no hint, therefore, in any of these texts, that the biblical writers viewed anything other than the written Word of God (the Old Testament) as the only infallible guide or authoritative source for the faith and practice of the church (in Armstrong, 237-238).

This perspective is quite interesting, seeing that what Jesus did in that verse was to encourage submission to the teaching of the Pharisees (not the Old Testament), and on the basis of their sitting on Moses' seat — a phrase not even found in the Old Testament, as James White admitted earlier.

In addition, White asserts, "We are only speaking of a position that existed at this time in the synagogue worship of the day" (White, 100). That is hardly "Old Testament alone." White's and Riddlebarger's positions here mutually exclude each other. Such

confusion is one of the hallmarks of an incoherent, weakly supported position.

Moreover, the Pharisees themselves can be dated only to the
second century B.C. at the earliest (see Douglas, 981) — long after the completion of the Old Testament. And they accepted the
full authority of oral tradition, as mentioned above.

Riddlebarger's argument, therefore, collapses on all points. He
cites Jesus' injunction to obey a group that began in the second
century B.C. — one that believes in oral tradition — and on the
basis of an institution of authority (Moses' seat) that cannot be
found in the Old Testament, as somehow the same as obeying
the letter of the Old Testament, which alone Jesus supposedly
regarded as authoritative. The internal inconsistency and incoherence of this position is surely evident.

Chapter Four

The Papacy

ST. PETER AS THE ROCK AND POSSESSOR
OF THE KEYS OF THE KINGDOM

Matthew 16:18-19: "And I tell you, you are Peter, and on this rock I will build my church, and the powers of death shall not prevail against it. I will give you the keys of the kingdom of heaven, and whatever you bind on earth shall be bound in heaven."

Isaiah 22:20-22: "In that day I will call my servant Eliakim the son of Hilkiah . . . and he shall be a father to the inhabitants of Jerusalem and to the house of Judah. And I will place on his shoulder the key of the house of David; he shall open, and none shall shut; and he shall shut, and none shall open."

Many Protestants are uncomfortable with Matthew 16:18-19, first because of its extraordinary implications for St. Peter's preeminence as the supreme earthly head of the Church, or Pope, which he was appointed by our Lord Jesus himself. The Church, according to Jesus (and in the Catholic view), is built upon Peter. In the figure and leadership of Peter in the Bible, the Catholic Church sees a primitive (later highly developed) model for Church government and papal headship. The Pope is not an autocrat or a dictator, but the "servant of the servants of God."

Furthermore, the passage also expresses *indefectibility*: the idea that the (institutional, historical) Church founded by Jesus can never be overcome by the powers of darkness; that it will always preserve the true Christian teaching handed down by Jesus to the Apostles.

Martin Luther, John Calvin, and a great number of Protestants through the centuries have held that the Catholic Church (led by the Pope) fell away from biblical truth at some point in the Middle Ages, became hopelessly corrupt due to the traditions of men, and lost the gospel of grace. What was once the Church ceased to be so, and a new entity had to come and take its place. But this passage mitigates against such an understanding (see also John 16:13). The Church cannot be so easily overcome.

Historically, the standard polemical response of Protestants to the phraseology of *rock* was to contend that it referred only to Peter's *faith*, not Peter himself. In that way, the institutional element of the charge from the Lord to St. Peter is avoided. If faith is the exclusive key to the meaning, then Peter can be viewed as merely a representative of a general principle, rather than unique in the sense of institutional, concrete leadership and jurisdiction. Thus John Calvin comments, "[N]othing is here given to Peter that was not common to him with his colleagues" (*Institutes*, IV, 6, 4).

This, if true, would undermine the Catholic claim to authority and tie into the Protestant notion of priesthood of all believers. Thus, along these lines, Ephesians 2:19-22 is often cited as a cross-reference, because it refers to the "household of God, built upon the foundation of the apostles and prophets, Christ Jesus himself being the cornerstone . . . in whom you also are built."

Jesus — so the argument goes — is the cornerstone, rather than Peter; all believers form the foundation, and the Church is egalitarian rather than hierarchical and episcopal (that is, with bishops and authority from the top down). Evangelical Protestantism today exhibits a variety of forms of church government, but what they all have in common is a rejection of the papacy. To greater or lesser degrees, they are variants of the ultimate primacy of the individual (private judgment) over that of an authoritative, hierarchical Church headed by a pope. Calvin observes, accordingly:

> [T]hey would have one man to preside over the whole Church, seeing the Church can never be without a head. . . . I am not unaware of the caviling objection which they are wont to urge — viz. that Christ is properly called the only Head, because he alone reigns by his own authority and in his own name; but that there is nothing in this to prevent what they call another *ministerial* head from being under him, and acting as his substitute. But this cavil cannot avail them, until they previously show that this office was ordained by Christ. . . . Scripture testifies that Christ is Head, and claims this honor for himself alone, it ought not to be transferred to any other than him whom Christ himself has made his vicegerent. But not only is there no passage to this effect, but it can be amply refuted by many passages (*Institutes*, IV, 6, 9).

Yet Jesus did not tell anyone *else* that He would build His Church upon them. He renamed no one else "Rock," and only one person received the "keys of the kingdom of heaven." Peter was unique in all these respects.

Somewhat surprisingly, the consensus among Protestant commentators today (including such eminent scholars such as R. T. France, D. A. Carson, William Hendriksen, Gerhard Maier, and Craig L. Blomberg), is that *rock* indeed refers to Peter himself, not his faith. They try to evade any further "Catholic" implication, though, by denying the notion of papal succession — that Peter as *rock* applies to Peter alone.

Other common Protestant arguments include the claim that the Petrine headship indicated in this passage has nothing to do with universal jurisdiction, or Roman primacy, or papal infallibility. But that is moving far ahead of the game. Systematic theology is built upon many strands of biblical evidences.

Here we are concerned with St. Peter as the proclaimed leader of the Church. The finer points and particulars of such an office require another discussion entirely. Scarcely any biblical passages contain a fully developed doctrine. That is as true of the papacy and ecclesiology as it is of any Christian theological construct.

In any event, papal succession is easily deduced from Matthew 16:18-19. St. Peter was the first leader of the Church. He died as the bishop in Rome (where St. Paul also died). That is how and why Roman primacy began: because Peter's successor was the bishop in the location where he ended up and died.

Moreover, if there was a leader of the Church in the beginning, it stands to reason that there would *continue* to be one (and that this was the will of God), just as George Washington, the first President of the United States when the presidency was established at the Constitutional Convention in 1787, was not intended to be the first and last president. Why have one president and then cease to have one thereafter and let the executive branch of government exist without a leader (or eliminate that office altogether)? Catholics are therefore simply applying common sense: if this is how Jesus set up the government of his Church in the beginning, then it seems obvious that it ought to continue perpetually in like fashion. But John Calvin did not see this at all:

> But were I to concede to them what they ask with regard to Peter — viz. that he was the chief of the apostles, and surpassed the others in dignity — there is no ground for

making a universal rule out of a special example, or wresting a single fact into a perpetual enactment, seeing that the two things are widely different (*Institutes*, IV, 6, 8).

Apostolic succession (contra Calvin) is also a biblical concept. After Judas betrayed our Lord, the remaining eleven disciples chose his successor, Matthias (Acts 1:20-26). St. Paul, likewise, passes on his *office* to Timothy (2 Timothy 4:1-6). Apostolic succession was a belief held from the beginning in the Church, and throughout the centuries, until Protestantism denied it. The Church Fathers made it a central criterion for the determination of what was truly Christian (orthodox) Tradition. If a doctrine could not be traced back to Jesus, it was suspect.

The phrase "keys of the kingdom of heaven" is worthy of a lengthy treatment, but we can only briefly touch upon it for our present purposes. Many Protestant commentators (contra Calvin's "apostolic egalitarianism") take the position that this phrase refers to the Old Testament office of *steward:* a type of governor or prime minister in the royal household, citing Isaiah 22:20-22 as a cross-reference.

This office carried a "daunting degree of authority" (R. T. France, 256). William F. Albright described Peter's role as "the same authority as that vested in the vizier, the master of the house, the chamberlain, of the royal household in ancient Israel" (Albright, 196), while the great Bible scholar F. F. Bruce noted that "in the new community which Jesus was about to build, Peter would be, so to speak, chief steward" (Bruce, 144).

Nevertheless, even some of these commentators move away from the seemingly clear implications of such a strong leadership in the Church by arguing (like Calvin) that this office was characterized primarily by the power to "bind and loose," a power that was granted also to the other disciples (Matt. 18:17-18; John 20:23).

This objection, is, I think, easily overcome by noting that there was only one *chief* steward of the kingdom, and that was Peter. When he, and his successors, bind and loose (rabbinical terms meaning to oblige obedience in some respect and to release one from it), it applies, or *can* apply, under certain conditions, to the entire Church, whereas the other disciples have only a limited sphere of authority.

If any one disciple is to be regarded as preeminent over all (from the biblical indications), then the choice could only be St. Peter, whom even Calvin grants an "honor of rank" and of "preeminence" but not of power or jurisdiction (*Institutes*, IV, 6, 5).

Another mistake lies in assuming that the holder of the "keys" has no further power beyond binding and loosing. For apart from that particular power, he remains preeminent in authority. Thus, the standard reference work *The New Bible Dictionary* (Douglas, 1018) describes this "power of the keys" as having to do with "ecclesiastical discipline" and "administrative authority [Isa. 22:22] with regard to the requirements of the household of faith," as well as "use of censures, excommunication, and absolution."

Protestant commentators have come a long way toward the Catholic view of Petrine primacy, but they usually leave out one or more crucial element of papal power and jurisdiction. The Catholic view alone explains all these implications and aspects (exegetical, legal, and historical) in a coherent way, by holding that Peter was both the leader of the early Church and a role model for future leaders who would assume his office through apostolic succession.

The ongoing internal Protestant disagreements regarding the nature of Church government offer yet another indication of the shortcomings and flaws of Protestantism, and its natural tendencies toward sectarianism and division. It is not insignificant that the historical papacy and primacy of Rome were significant factors in the Church universal right from the start, with the martyrdoms of St. Peter and St. Paul in Rome and the writings of St. Clement of Rome, who took it upon himself authoritatively to instruct other churches. In great figures such as Pope St. Leo the Great (ruled 440-461) and Pope St. Gregory the Great (ruled 590-604), all the essentials of the modern papacy are already abundantly present and visible. The passages under consideration here provide the biblical foundation for these views.

Protestantism, on the other hand, not only eliminated the historical papacy, which was hugely important in Church history for 1,500 years; it also ditched apostolic succession and, for the most part, councils and even bishops. Thus it is in a radical discontinuity with Christian precedent as well as with Scripture. For the Fathers, this would have been sufficient to establish a serious, grave doubt as to the authority of Protestantism over against Catholicism.

Insofar as Protestantism continues to claim to be reforming the Church universal and returning to the beliefs and practices of the early Church (which was presupposed in the terminology of "Reformation"), this is a huge difficulty. The clearest evidence from the Bible, as well as the historical facts concerning the early Church (and even the medieval Church) simply are much more in accord with Catholic belief and structure than any form of Protestantism.

Chapter Five

Justification and Salvation

FAITH AND WORKS: TWO SIDES OF ONE COIN

James 2:24: "You see that a man is justified by works and not by faith alone" (cf. 1:22, 2:14, 17, 20, 22, 26).

Catholics believe in an organic relationship between faith and works. Far from being intractably opposed to one another, they are in fact inseparable. Faith is necessary to produce truly good works, and works in turn are the evidence of a true faith. This verse would appear, on the other hand, to present a problem for the fundamental Protestant notion of *sola fide*, or faith alone. The Bible here expresses precisely the opposite proposition: one is *not* justified by faith alone.

Much of the Protestant polemic historically has been oriented toward "faith alone," and a false charge that the Catholic Church asserts salvation through works. It is no small wonder, then, that verses such as this one make Protestants squirm. Protestants must provide an explanation for this verse and related ones that escapes the straightforward, literal meaning.

We can be fairly sure that if the passage had stated the *opposite* — "a man is justified by faith alone," an idea that never appears in a single verse in Holy Scripture, nor is it taught in the

Bible as a whole — it would have been one of the centerpieces of the Protestant apologetic. But since the verse flatly contradicts one of their major premises, Protestants are forced to come up with tortured explanations or else ignore it altogether.

The common Protestant reply to James 2:24 (and the book of James in general) is to say that a different sense of the word *justified* is being employed by St. James. He is referring to the *fruit* of justification and the merely *outward* indication that one is saved. Catholics, on the other hand, follow St. Augustine's understanding of merit:

> What merit of man is there before grace by which he can achieve grace, as only grace works every one of our good merits in us, and as God, when He crowns our merits, crowns nothing else but His own gifts? (Ep. 194, 5, 19; in Ott, 265).

But these two clashing approaches to justification have a substantial meeting point: both accept the notion of *sola gratia,* or salvation by grace alone (over against the heresy of Pelagianism, which holds that man can be saved by works or his own self-generated effort). Both also believe that good works are necessary in the Christian life.

Catholics believe that faith and works are more closely tied together, and related to justification itself. Works can follow only by God's grace and do not cause salvation, but they must be present, because (per James), "faith apart from works is dead" (James 2:26).

In large part, the Protestant-Catholic dispute is over the distinction between justification (that is, salvation) and sanctification (holiness). Protestants believe that the latter has nothing whatsoever to do with justification (which is imputed to the believer or declared by God), yet that it should follow from it. Catholics think they are closely related. The practical result is arguably the same in either system. Classical Protestantism will not accept a person as "saved" if that person shows no fruit of good works in his life. They will deny that he ever was saved if he habitually engages in serious sin. Both Luther and Calvin taught this. Luther wrote (contrary to much Evangelical talk today):

> We must therefore certainly maintain that where there is no faith there also can be no good works; and conversely, that there is no faith where there are no good works. Therefore faith and good works should be so closely joined together that the essence of the entire Christian life consists in both (in Althaus, 246).
>
> Accordingly, if good works do not follow, it is certain that this faith in Christ does not dwell in our heart, but dead faith (in Althaus, 246; also LW, 34, 111; cf. 34, 161).

St. James is emphasizing the works element of salvation, and St. Paul, the faith element. But neither denies the other element (see in Paul, e.g., Rom. 2:5-13; 1 Cor. 3:8-9; Eph. 2:10; Titus 3:8). Neither James nor Paul compartmentalizes works and faith into distinct theological constructs of "sanctification" and "justification." Rather, what is seen here is an organic unity, precisely as in the Catholic view.

But many Protestants whom I have come across think that the Bible distinguishes here between justification *before* God and justification *before men*. Their argument hinges on a different sense of justification in James compared with the rest of Holy Scripture.

Catholics believe that salvation is an ongoing endeavor, not a one-time event, as Protestants think (see, e.g., 1 Cor. 9:27, 10:12; Phil. 2:12-13, 3:11-14; Heb. 3:12-14). Obviously, if it were an instantaneous event, there would be no time for works at all, so works are irrelevant and meaningless in any discussion of justification in *that* sense. James is discussing justification-in-process. Ironically, Luther himself seemed to believe in ongoing justification:

Our justification is not yet finished. It is in the process of being made; it is neither something which is actually completed nor is it essentially present. It is still under construction (in Althaus, 245).

On the other hand, at certain points in his life, Luther was willing to disavow the canonicity of James. Paul Althaus noted how Luther believed that even some passages in the Bible cease to "have the authority of the word of God" if they "cannot be unified with the witness of all the rest of Scripture." Thus, Luther wrote in 1543, three years before his death:

Away with James. . . . His authority is not great enough to cause me to abandon the doctrine of faith and to deviate from the authority of the other apostles and the entire Scripture (in Althaus, 81).

The year before, Luther had written:

Up to this point I have been accustomed to deal with and interpret [James] according to the sense of the rest of Scripture. For you will judge that none of it must be set forth contrary to manifest Holy Scripture. Accordingly, if they will not agree to my interpretations, then I shall make rubble of it. I almost feel like throwing Jimmy into the stove (in Althaus, 81; LW, 34, 317).

In his preface to the New Testament, written in 1522, Luther famously described James as "an epistle of straw" (see Bainton, 259). He did not consider it the true writing of an apostle (even in 1545, the year before his death). In his revised version of his preface to the book, he stated that it taught works-righteousness, "rends" the Scripture, and "resists" St. Paul.

Luther was equally strident when defending his addition of the word *alone* after *faith* in Romans 3:28:

Thus I will have it, thus I order it, my will is reason enough. . . . Luther will have it so, and . . . he is a Doctor above all Doctors in the whole of Popery (in O'Connor, 25; Letter to Wenceslaus Link in 1530).

Obviously, if the book of James did not make Protestants (perhaps Luther, above all) squirm, they would not be led to adopt such desperate measures and arguments to explain it (away, as it were). Thus, I once had an Internet dialogue with a person who constructed his entire exegetical argument from James's use of the word *see* in this verse. He reasoned that James was referring simply to *outward manifestations* of true saving faith, which came by faith alone, because this was what other human beings could *see*.

I doubt that this is a very common Protestant interpretation of the verse, especially among scholars, but it does in any event illustrate the extent to which even thoughtful, intelligent Protestants (and this person was pretty sharp) will go to explain the difficult passages of James that seem to contradict their theology.

This argument (and, more important, the sophisticated version of it that does not depend on the words "you see") collapses utterly, however, in light of a rather simple contextual consideration. James 2:21, three verses before, reads, "Was not Abraham our father justified by works, when he offered his son Isaac upon the altar?" This justification was not "before men," but before the Lord. Yet Scripture teaches us that Abraham was justified in that very act, even though no other human being was around to see it.

That is not to say that his faith was not important. His act of obedience displayed great faith — a faith inseparably united with his actions. In fact, the very next verse (James 2:22) gives us exactly this authoritative interpretation: "You see that faith was active along with his works, and faith was completed by works." The real clincher, however, comes in verse 2:23: "and the scripture was fulfilled which says, 'Abraham believed God, and it was reckoned to him as righteousness.' "

Note what has occurred here. If the fulfillment of Abraham's "faith alone" act of "believing in God" came via a *work*, which no one else saw, two things logically follow:

1. Faith and works are shown once again to be two sides of a coin. They cannot be, and should not be, separated. St. Paul's "belief reckoned as righteousness" is grounded in a work, and authoritatively so, since one apostle interprets the same passage that another has interpreted, based on an Old Testament passage. Inspired — God-breathed — Scripture cannot contradict itself.

2. The Protestant "faith alone" concept that is built upon the Abrahamic verses having to do with faith, among others, cannot possibly be interpreted as excluding works altogether (that is, from justification). It simply cannot be done.

In popular Protestant understanding, the radical dichotomy of "faith versus works" largely dominates. This is unbiblical, as I think can be demonstrated in the commentary above and in a close examination of related passages such as those that follow.

THE RICH YOUNG RULER'S
QUESTION ABOUT SALVATION

Luke 18:18-25: "And a ruler asked him, 'Good teacher, what shall I do to inherit eternal life?' And Jesus said to him, 'Why do you call me good? No one is good but God alone. You know the commandments: "Do not commit adultery. Do not kill. Do not steal. Do not bear false witness. Honor your father and mother." ' And he said, 'All these I have observed from my youth.' And when Jesus heard it, he said to him, 'One thing you still lack. Sell all that you have and distribute to the poor, and you will have treasure in heaven; and come, follow me.' But when he heard this he became sad, for he was very rich. Jesus looking at him said, 'How hard it is for those who have riches to enter the kingdom of God! For it is easier for a camel to go through the eye of a needle than for a rich man to enter the kingdom of God.' "

Protestants (broadly speaking) deny that works have anything to do with salvation (justification). Catholics believe that faith and works are inextricably tied together in an organic relationship (as are justification and sanctification, which are both ongoing processes). As I have often commented in the course of my apologetics endeavors: this passage and many others like it do not read the way one would (all things being equal) *expect* them to read, if indeed distinctive Protestant theology is true. Once in a while, it is instructive, and fun, to engage in some hypothetical Bible translation, in order to make the Bible conform more closely to the Evangelical Protestant outlook. This passage is ripe for "new and improved" translation. Let us see how the Revised Evangelical Version (REV) might render it:

Luke 18:18-25 (REV): "And a ruler asked him, 'Good teacher, what shall I believe to inherit eternal life?' And Jesus said to him, 'Why do you call me good? No one is good but God alone. You know the commandments: "Do not commit adultery. Do not kill. Do not steal. Do not bear false witness. Honor your father and mother." ' And he said, 'All these I have observed from my youth.' And when Jesus heard it, he said to him, 'One thing you still lack. Know that the commandments have nothing to do with your salvation because they concern works. Have faith alone in me alone, and you will have treasure in heaven; and come, follow me.' But when he heard

> this he became sad, for he lacked faith alone. Jesus looking at him said, 'How hard it is for those who lack faith alone in me alone to enter the kingdom of God! For it is easier for a camel to go through the eye of a needle than for a man who lacks faith alone in me alone to enter the kingdom of God.' "

The Protestant constantly cries, "Faith alone!" Yet the Bible does not communicate the gospel or saving faith in those terms. Faith cannot be separated from works. We have seen this clearly in our treatment of James 2:24.

In any event, despite the nuances and deeper understanding of scholars, at the popular level Protestants often create a complete dichotomy between faith and works. One gets the impression that if they could somehow go back to the first century and be apostles and disciples of Jesus, they would have written a Bible vastly different from the one we possess.

Catholics refuse to separate faith and works, while asserting together with Protestants (it can never be stressed or repeated enough) that grace alone is the cause, ground, and ultimate source of our salvation and justification.

GOD'S FELLOW WORKERS?

1 Corinthians 3:8-9: "He who plants and he who waters are equal, and each shall receive his wages according to his labor. For we are *God's fellow workers;* you are God's field, God's building."

1 Corinthians 15:10: "But by the grace of God I am what I am, and his grace toward me was not in vain. On the contrary, I worked harder than any of them, though it was not I, but the grace of God which is with me."

2 **Corinthians 6:1:** "Working together with him, then, we entreat you not to accept the grace of God in vain."

2 **Peter 1:10:** "Therefore, brethren, be the more zealous to confirm your call and election, for if you do this you will never fall."

These verses have to do with the controversy among Christians concerning human free will, and whether the belief in cooperation with God, entirely enabled by his grace, amounts to works-salvation. Catholics accept this cooperation, as explicitly described in Holy Scripture. Protestants (particularly Calvinists) deny that this kind of cooperation takes place or that it has anything whatsoever to do with salvation. They deride it as "synergism," an arrangement in which man is saved partly by grace and partly by his own efforts.

Louis Bouyer, a convert to Catholicism from Lutheranism, a prominent liturgist, and the author of many books, explains how Catholics view the Pauline notion of God's fellow workers:

> The profound assertion of the total causality of grace in salvation requires that both the good works following on grace, and the faith which receives it, are its product. . . . The assertion that, in salvation, all is the work of grace . . . is precisely what is affirmed by the genuine Catholic tradition. . . .
>
> [St. Paul] himself tells us to "work out your salvation with fear and trembling," at the very moment when he affirms that "knowing that it is God who works in you both to will and to accomplish. . . ." [G]race is not opposed to human acts and endeavor in order to attain salvation, but arouses them and exacts their performance. . . . [I]n one sense God does all, and in another man must do all, for he has to make everything his own; but he cannot — he can

do absolutely nothing valid for salvation, except in complete dependence on grace (Bouyer, 52-53, 143, 157).

John Calvin expresses remarkable agreement with Catholic theology in this respect. Ironically, he interprets passages like those above in the same fashion as Catholics, but is unaware that Catholics do not disagree. In a study of how Protestants try to explain away biblical passages, I think it is good to include a few examples of how Protestants mistakenly think Catholics are doing the same, whereas in fact the two parties do not substantially disagree. For example, in his *Commentaries* (at 1 Cor. 3:9) Calvin blatantly misrepresents Catholic teaching:

[W]hile God could accomplish the work entirely himself, he calls us, puny mortals, to be as it were his coadjutors, and makes use of us as instruments. As to the perversion of this statement by the Papists, for supporting their system of free will, it is beyond measure silly, for Paul shows here, not what men can effect by their natural powers, but what the Lord accomplishes through means of them by his grace.

Calvin's caricature is not Catholic teaching at all. Catholics do not believe men can do any good "by their natural powers," nor do we deny *sola gratia* in the slightest. Simply cooperating with the grace is not "human generation"; it is God generation. The Council of Trent is very clear on this:

Canon I on Justification: "If anyone saith that man may be justified before God by his own works, whether done through the teaching of human nature, or that of the law, without the grace of God through Jesus Christ; let him be anathema."

Chapter VIII on Justification: "[N]one of those things which precede justification — whether faith or works — merit the grace itself of justification. For if it be a grace, it is not now by works; otherwise, as the same Apostle says, grace is no more grace."

ST. PAUL'S PLEA: "WORK OUT YOUR SALVATION"

Philippians 2:12-13: "Therefore, my beloved, as you have always obeyed, so now, not only as in my presence but much more in my absence, work out your own salvation with fear and trembling; for God is at work in you, both to will and to work for his good pleasure."

Catholics assert that passages such as this one teach that God's free grace can be made "both to will and to work" in us. It is not self-generated by us; it is a gift of God. On the popular level, many Protestants accuse Catholics of falsely using this verse to assert a salvation by works. They wrongly think that Catholicism teaches a salvation by self-generated works, rather than merely acknowledging the necessary place of works, which are themselves entirely the cause and result of God's grace (as indicated in the verse above by the clause "God is at work in you"). Calvin again falls prey to the temptation to war against straw men, in his *Commentaries*, for this verse:

As Pelagians of old, so Papists at this day make a proud boast of this passage, with the view of extolling man's excellence. . . . Inasmuch, then, as the work is ascribed to God and man in common, they assign the half to each.

Of course, Catholics have done no such thing. We do not claim that salvation is a half-and-half proposition. Catholics accept the plain meaning of this passage: we cooperate with God, but in the end, it is *God* who does all, since he is "at work" in us, "both to will and to work." Calvin is simply unable to grasp this biblical paradox. For him it is either/or : if God does all, man must do nothing. Conversely, if man does anything, then this is works-salvation and contrary to grace. But the Bible does not require this choice. Grace does all, and man also *cooperates* with it.

In two sermons (one on this very passage), John Wesley, the great evangelist and founder of Methodism, expresses thoughts very similar to Louis Bouyer's. Again, we observe that there need be no significant difference between mainstream (Arminian) Protestantism and Catholicism with regard to the place of works in the scheme of salvation:

> Neither is salvation of the works we do when we believe; for it is then God that worketh in us: and therefore, that He giveth us a reward for what He Himself worketh.
>
> God works in us — therefore man *can* work. . . . God works in you — therefore you *must* work. You must work together with Him, or He will cease working ("Salvation by Faith," 1738; "On Working Out Our Own Salvation," 1788; in Lindstrom, 92, 215).

OBEDIENCE NECESSARY FOR SALVATION

Hebrews 5:9: "And being made perfect he became the source of eternal salvation to all who obey him."

Catholics point out that obedience to God is directly tied into salvation (as opposed to a "bare assent" being all that is necessary to receive this salvation). This verse would make many Protestants squirm, for it states outright that salvation involves *obeying*, not merely *believing* (which is basically what the Protestant notion of *sola fide* is about). The REV Bible would read, accordingly, "all who have *faith alone* in him."

Most Protestants place the elements of obedience, holiness, and righteous conduct under the classification of *sanctification:*

distinct, in a separate, airtight compartment, from justification and salvation. They believe justification occurs in an instant (this is where a man gets "saved"), but that sanctification has nothing to do with justification. It should normally follow, but, strictly speaking, it is not *necessary* for salvation. Hebrews 5:9 appears to be straightforwardly at variance with that view.

The Methodist expositor Adam Clarke, in his commentary on this verse, essentially agrees with the Catholic position, because Methodist soteriology (theology of salvation) and its conception of sanctification is virtually the same as in Catholic theology:

> It is not merely believers, but obedient believers, that shall be finally saved. Therefore this text is an absolute, unimpeachable evidence, that it is not the imputed obedience of Christ that saves any man.

Curiously, Luther and Calvin both casually equate obedience in this verse with faith:

> As many as are saved are drawn by this power through the revelation of Christ, and cleave to Christ by faith. For this cleaving to Christ is that which is referred to when it speaks of "all that obey him" (in Atkinson, 116; *Lectures on the Epistle to the Hebrews*, 1517-1518).

> [B]y saying this he recommends faith to us; for he becomes not ours, nor his blessings, except as far as we receive them and him by faith (Calvin's *Commentaries*; on Hebrews 5:9).

I find this somewhat amusing. Luther and Calvin believe that faith alone saves a person, and works or obedience have nothing whatsoever to do with it — not even an obedience necessarily made possible entirely by grace. So, when faced with a verse that clearly states a contrary proposition, they simply proclaim that obedience is, in fact, just another way of describing faith, and presto! — the apparent contradiction vanishes. Yet no one seems to notice the sleight-of-hand.

DISOBEDIENCE LED TO DEATH, OBEDIENCE TO JUSTIFICATION

Romans 5:17-19: "If, because of one man's trespass, death reigned through that one man, much more will those who receive the abundance of grace and the free gift of righteousness reign in life through the one man Jesus Christ. Then as one man's trespass led to condemnation for all men, so one man's act of righteousness leads to acquittal and life for all men. For as by one man's disobedience many were made sinners, so by one man's obedience many will be made righteous."

This passage presents, upon deeper inspection, a subtle but effective argument for actual, infused, intrinsic justification (the Catholic view), as opposed to the Protestants' extrinsic, imputed, merely "declared" righteousness. In other words, for Catholics, justification causes an actual, observable change in a person and has to do with holiness and righteousness. The Protestant view, on the other hand, holds that God declares a person justified and righteous, even if there is no outward change in him.

Note the parallelism in verse 19 between those who are "made sinners" and those who are "made righteous." Protestants agree that original sin is actual: the sin is *real*, not just declared. Therefore, it stands to reason that men are "made righteous" in the same fashion: the righteousness is real, not just declared and imputed by God.

Commentators Robert Jamieson, A. R. Fausset, and David Brown, authors of a widely used nineteenth-century *Commentary on the Whole Bible*, provide an example of how Protestants wrongly interpret this passage:

> The significant word twice rendered, *made*, does not signify to *work a change upon* a person or thing, but to *constitute* or *ordain*, as will be seen from all the places where it is used. Here, accordingly, it is intended to express that *judicial act* which holds men, in virtue of their connection with Adam, as sinners; and, in connection with Christ, as righteous.

Now, the Greek word here for *make* is *kathisteemi*. It is often used in the New Testament in the sense of "making a ruler [of a people]" (see Matt. 24:45, 25:21; Luke 12:42; Acts 7:10, 27, 35). It is also used in the sense of *ordain* or *appoint* (see Acts 6:3; Titus 1:5; Heb. 5:1, 8:3). In James 3:6 and 4:4 in the RSV, it is simply translated *is* (in a quite literal sense). The parallelism of these uses, then, according to the argument by Jamieson, Fausset, and Brown, would be as follows:

1. Made a ruler.
2. Ordained an elder.
3. Made sinners.
4. Made righteous.

The claim was that these instances of being "made" or "ordained" did not change the person; they were judicial declarations. This ties in, of course, with the Protestant conception of declared, extrinsic, imputed justification. God declares men righteous on the basis of the shed blood of Christ, but they are not *really* righteous — or at least not in the sense that it has anything to do with their salvation; righteousness is relegated to a nonsalvific category of sanctification.

However, being appointed a ruler or elder in a church does indeed have *concrete and visible effects*, not simply declared ones, although the person remains exactly the same. Having attained to that office, a ruler is different from what he was before.

The President of the United States is a different man from what he was before he became President. He has various powers and duties and so forth. It is not as if a ruler is declared to be so and then nothing happens and life goes on as it did before. The person *becomes* a ruler or an elder.

In the same manner, the person who is "made righteous" *is* different, not merely *declared* to be so, just as when the human race fell, men were really made sinners; they were different from what they had been before. This interpretation seems more plausible and straightforward, at any rate, than the Protestant attempt to read its distinctive soteriology into the text.

Presbyterian Albert Barnes, in his *Notes,* another very popular nineteenth-century commentary, clearly indicates in his remarks for this verse that when referring to the results of the Fall, to the human race made sinful, the term *made (kathisteemi)* is not to be interpreted in the sense of "imputed":

> [I]t means to *become,* to be in fact, etc. James 3:6, "So *is* the tongue among our members," etc. That is, it becomes such. James 4:4, "The friendship of the world *is* enmity with God"; it *becomes* such; it is in fact thus, and is thus to be regarded. . . . There is not the slightest intimation that it was by imputation. . . . [T]he object of the apostle is not to show that they were charged with the sin of another, but that they were in fact *sinners* themselves.

But Presbyterian theology (and much of Protestant theology, generally speaking) fails to see that it *also* does not mean "imputed" when it is referring to the results of the Redemption, to those "made righteous." John Henry Newman, on the other hand, in his Anglican period, grasped the full implication of the passage:

> Sin, which we derive through Adam, is not a name merely, but a dreadful reality; and so our new righteousness also is a

real and not a merely imputed righteousness. It is real righteousness, because it comes from the Holy and Divine Spirit, who vouchsafes, in our Church's language, to pour his gift into our hearts, and who thus makes us acceptable to God, whereas by nature, on account of original sin, we are displeasing to him (*Parochial and Plain Sermons,* V, 1840, Sermon 11: "The Law of the Spirit," 1041-1053).

ST. PAUL ON FALLING AWAY
FROM THE FAITH AND SALVATION

1 Corinthians 9:27: "I pommel my body and subdue it, lest after preaching to others I myself should be disqualified."

1 Corinthians 10:12: "Therefore let anyone who thinks that he stands take heed lest he fall."

Galatians 5:1: "For freedom Christ has set us free; stand fast, therefore, and do not submit again to a yoke of slavery."

Galatians 5:4: "You are severed from Christ, you who would be justified by the law; you have fallen away from grace."

Philippians 3:8-14: "Indeed I count everything as loss because of the surpassing worth of knowing Christ Jesus my Lord. For his sake I have suffered the loss of all things, and count them as refuse, in order that I may gain Christ and be found in him, not having a righteousness of my own, based on law, but that which is through faith in Christ, the righteousness from God that depends on faith; that I may know him and the power of his resurrection, and may share his sufferings, becoming like him in his death, that if possible I may attain the resurrection from the dead. Not that I have already obtained this or am already perfect; but I press on to make it my own, because Christ Jesus has made me his own. Brethren, I do not consider that I have made it my own; but one thing I do, forgetting what lies behind and straining forward to what lies ahead, I press on toward the goal for the prize of the upward call of God in Christ Jesus."

1 Timothy 4:1: "Now the Spirit expressly says that in later times some will depart from the faith by giving heed to deceitful spirits and doctrines of demons."

Catholics believe, in accordance with these passages, that salvation can be lost and that one can fall out of faith and the good graces of God. Passages such as these about falling away from faith, or what is called *apostasy*, present a problem, however, for Calvinist Protestants, because their system requires them to deny the possibility that such a thing can ever take place. For them, sinners are elected by God from eternity and protected from ever falling away. Human participation or vigilance or effort plays no role whatsoever in ultimate salvation.

Therefore, the elect or "saved" person cannot possibly lose his salvation. When a person seems to be on the wrong path (caught up in adultery or some other clearly sinful behavior), the Calvinist community immediately assumes that he was never saved in the first place (or else he would not have sinned so badly). This is circular reasoning, and also contrary to much Scripture, such as the verses above.

Albert Barnes, in his *Notes*, makes a fallacious analysis of Galatians 5:4. He tries to apply Paul's words about apostasy to those who never possessed grace to begin with, since they were (like the Judaizers) trying to be saved by the law:

[T]his passage does not prove that anyone who has ever been a true Christian has fallen away. The fair interpretation of the passage does not demand that. Its simple and obvious meaning is that, if a man who had been a professed Christian *should be* justified by his own conformity to the law, and adopt that mode of justification, then that would amount to a rejection of the mode of salvation by Christ, and would be a renouncing of the plan of justification by grace.

This makes no sense and, with all due respect to Barnes, cannot be sustained from the text. The fact remains that these people fell away. Whether they fell away from a belief-system of justification by grace or from grace as a state of personal relationship with God, or both, makes no difference. For in both instances, they were either believing as Christians are, or in the state of grace and regeneration that Christians are in, by virtue of baptism and the personal decision to follow Christ.

Secondly, the entire tone and tenor of the epistle to the Galatians shows that Paul believes he is writing to Christians. He refers to "the churches of Galatia" (1:2). In 1:6 he speaks of the Galatians "deserting him who called you in the grace of Christ and turning to a different gospel." This does not read as if they never knew or believed in God's grace. One cannot desert something he never had. One cannot turn to something different if one never possessed the thing that is being contrasted with the different thing.

If St. Paul thought they had never possessed the true gospel in the first place, it seems obvious that he would have used different terminology; he would have written that they never *did* understand or accept the gospel of grace alone. He would not have expressed his judgment in terms of deserting and turning and falling away and being "severed from Christ." Can a branch be severed from a tree to which it was never attached?

St. Paul assumes throughout that this was a case of apostasy of those who were Christians. He says they "received" the gospel (1:9); he refers to the "grace that was given to me" (2:9) and then says the Galatians had "begun with the Spirit" (3:3); he writes to them that "as many of you as were baptized into Christ have put on Christ. . . . You are all one in Christ Jesus" (3:27-28); he says the Galatians are God's "sons," upon whom He "sent the Spirit of his Son" into "*our* hearts, crying, 'Abba! Father!' " (4:6).

St. Paul states that they formerly did not know God, but "have come to know God" only to return to bondage again (4:8-9). He believes that the Galatians "were running well; who hindered you from obeying the truth [5:7]?" The entire letter explicitly indicates apostasy. It could hardly be more clear than it is. What else could Paul have written to make it any *more* obvious?

Thirdly, logically speaking, the fact that some might be turning to salvation by works and law does not prove that they *never* accepted salvation by grace alone. The two are not intrinsically related. Believing one thing does not prove that one never adhered to a different system formerly. Barnes simply assumes this (as is so often the case in Protestant exegesis — at least where "Catholic" implications are present), because he is not allowed to hold that anyone can ever fall away from faith, no matter what the Bible might inform us about such possibilities.

Fourthly, the Greek word for *fallen, ekpipto*, is often used elsewhere in the New Testament in the sense of "falling from that estate in which something once was"; for example: the stars from heaven (Mark 13:25); chains falling off hands (Acts 12:7); shipwreck and falling off a boat (Acts 27:26, 29, 32); and apostasy, or at least a spiritual degeneration (Rev. 2:5). Greek scholar Gerhard Kittel discusses the root word *pipto* in relation to apostasy:

[P]ipto may also be used for loss of faith and separation from grace (1 Cor. 10:12). At issue here is an apostasy from God or Christ which means disqualification (1 Cor. 9:27). In Rom. 14:4 standing and falling are oriented to the fact that each must answer to the Lord as Judge. The use is absolute in Heb. 4:11: a specific sin is not in view but apostasy. In Rev. 2:5 leaving the first love is the point (Kittel, 847).

Much more plausible is, I think, John Henry Newman's sermon on Philippians 3:12 and related scriptures:

[W]e do not know the *standard* by which God will judge us. Nothing that we are can assure us that we shall answer to what He expects of us; for we do not know what that is. . . . This thought will surely ever keep us from dwelling on our own proficiency. . . .

The doctrine, then, that few are chosen though many be called, properly understood, has no tendency whatever to make us fancy ourselves secure and others reprobate. We cannot see the heart; we can but judge from externals, from words and deeds, professions and habits. But these will not save us, unless we persevere in them to the end; and they are no evidence that we shall be saved, except so far as they suggest hope that we shall persevere. They are but a beginning; they tell for nothing till they are completed. Till we have done all, we have done nothing; we have but a prospect, not possession (*Parochial and Plain Sermons*, V, 1840, Sermon 18: "Many Called, Few Chosen," 1110-1119).

OTHER BIBLICAL WRITERS ON APOSTASY

Hebrews 3:12-14: "Take care, brethren, lest there be in any of you an evil, unbelieving heart, leading you to fall away from the living God. But exhort one another every day, as long as it is called 'today,' that none of you may be hardened by the deceitfulness of sin. For we share in Christ, if only we hold our first confidence firm to the end."

Hebrews 6:4-6: "For it is impossible to restore again to repentance those who have once been enlightened, who have tasted the heavenly gift, and have become partakers of the Holy Spirit, and have tasted the goodness of the word of God and the powers of the age to come, if they then commit apostasy, since they crucify the Son of God on their own account and hold him up to contempt."

2 Peter 2:15: "Forsaking the right way, they have gone astray; they have followed the way of Balaam, the son of Beor, who loved gain from wrongdoing."

2 Peter 2:20-22: "For if, after they have escaped the defilements of the world through the knowledge of our Lord and Savior Jesus Christ, they are again entangled in them and overpowered, the last state has become worse for them than the first. For it would have been better for them never to have known the way of righteousness than after knowing it to turn back from the holy commandment delivered to them. It has happened to them according to the true proverb, 'The dog turns back to his own vomit, and the sow is washed only to wallow in the mire.' "

John Calvin's treatment of Hebrews 6:4-6 in his *Commentaries* is a virtual case study of special pleading and drawing of arbitrary distinctions without a difference. His conclusions are not to be found in the biblical text at all, but he inserts his understanding into it, because his preconceived system *requires* him to do so. This is what is called *eisegesis*, or reading *into* the biblical text, rather than *out of* it (Protestants frequently accuse Catholics of this shortcoming). The fifty-cent word *reprobate* that he uses means one who is outside of the faith, or damned, or not one of the elect (to use common Calvinist terminology).

> I am aware that it seems unaccountable to some how faith is attributed to the reprobate, seeing that it is declared by Paul to be one of the fruits of election. Yet the difficulty is easily solved, for although none are enlightened into faith, and truly feel the efficacy of the gospel, with the exception of those who are fore-ordained to salvation, experience shows that the reprobate are sometimes affected in a way so similar to the elect that even in their own judgment there is no difference between them.

In other words, there is no way we can determine (or even make an educated guess) by any outward sign whether a person is truly a follower of Jesus and in his good graces! This is a radical principle that readily leads (in sinful human beings) to spiritual arrogance and elitism, because the means to determine whether one is "saved" or "justified" or "of the elect" are internal and subjective and tainted by our own natural bias toward ourselves, rather than outward and objective in a way that others can judge. Thus, the "full assurance" Calvin refers to in the following remark, becomes a rather empty, hollow concept:

> [T]hough there is a great resemblance and affinity between the elect of God and those who are impressed for a time with a fading faith, yet the elect alone have that full assurance.

The ostensible follower of Christ may fall away (even in Calvin's diluted sense) from the faith; in which case Calvin would simply proclaim that he never was a pre-ordained true believer to begin with. Therefore, it follows that no one can be assured of his salvation (contrary to Calvin's and Luther's assertions) at *any* time, since no one knows what will happen in the future to disqualify him from ever having been saved. This is a great weakness in Protestant soteriology, but to examine it fully is beyond our immediate purview.

Meanwhile, believers are taught to examine themselves carefully and humbly, lest carnal security creep in and take the place of assurance of faith.

But there cannot *be* any such assurance in Calvin's system! This is an unbiblical "faith in faith" or "faith in one's own certainty and 'assurance' " rather than faith in Jesus and the corresponding Pauline vigilance to maintain one's salvation — always by God's grace but not without human cooperation. Even a pardoned murderer has to accept the pardon from the governor and walk out of the prison.

The Bible could not be any more explicit about apostasy than it is in these passages, yet Calvin attempts to overcome all that by arbitrarily applying his preconceived system and denying the obvious meaning of everything that is written. It is a classic instance of eisegesis.

A straightforward reading of the text demonstrates clearly that these people did indeed fall away; that they were Christians — precisely the fact that is so alarming to St. Paul and causes him to write his letter in the first place.

Chapter Six

Judgment and Good Works

THE CRUCIAL ROLE OF WORKS (AND ABSENCE OF FAITH) IN JUDGMENT DAY ACCOUNTS

Matthew 7:16-27: "You will know them by their fruits. Are grapes gathered from thorns, or figs from thistles? So, every sound tree bears good fruit, but the bad tree bears evil fruit. A sound tree cannot bear evil fruit, nor can a bad tree bear good fruit. Every tree that does not bear good fruit is cut down and thrown into the fire. Thus you will know them by their fruits. Not every one who says to me, 'Lord, Lord,' shall enter the kingdom of heaven, but he who does the will of my Father who is in heaven. On that day many will say to me, 'Lord, Lord, did we not prophesy in your name, and cast out demons in your name, and do many mighty works in your name?' And then will I declare to them, 'I never knew you; depart from me, you evildoers.' Everyone, then, who hears these words of mine and does them will be like a wise man who built his house upon the rock; and the rain fell, and the floods came, and the winds blew and beat upon that house, but it did not fall, because it had been founded on the rock. And everyone who hears these words of mine and does not do them will be like a foolish man who built his house upon the sand; and the rain fell, and the floods came, and the winds blew and beat against that house, and it fell; and great was the fall of it."

Matthew 16:27: "For the Son of man is to come with his angels in the glory of his Father, and then he will repay every man for what he has done."

Matthew 25:31-46: "When the Son of man comes in his glory, and all the angels with him, then he will sit on his glorious throne. Before him will be gathered all the nations, and he will separate them one from another as a shepherd separates the sheep from the goats, and he will place the sheep at his right hand, but the goats at the left. Then the King will say to those at his right hand, 'Come, O blessed of my Father, inherit the kingdom prepared for you from the foundation of the world; for I was hungry and you gave me food, I was thirsty and you gave me drink, I was a stranger and you welcomed me, I was naked and you clothed me, I was sick and you visited me, I was in prison and you came to me.' Then the righteous will answer him, 'Lord, when did we see thee hungry and feed thee, or thirsty and give thee drink? And when did we see thee a stranger and welcome thee, or naked and clothe thee? And when did we see thee sick or in prison and visit thee?' And the King will answer them, 'Truly, I say to you, as you did it to one of the least of these my brethren, you did it to me.' Then he will say to those at his left hand, 'Depart from me, you cursed, into the eternal fire prepared for the devil and his angels; for I was hungry and you gave me no food, I was thirsty and you gave me no drink, I was a stranger and you did not welcome me, naked and you did not clothe me, sick and in prison and you did not visit me.' Then they also will answer, 'Lord, when did we see thee hungry or thirsty or a stranger or naked or sick or in prison, and did not minister to thee?' Then he will answer them, 'Truly, I say to you, as you did it not to one of the least of these, you did it not to me.' And they will go away into eternal punishment, but the righteous into eternal life."

2 Corinthians 5:10: "For we must all appear before the judgment seat of Christ, so that each one may receive good or evil, according to what he has done in the body."

1 Peter 1:17: "And if you invoke as Father him who judges each one impartially according to his deeds, conduct yourselves with fear throughout the time of your exile."

Revelation 22:12: "Behold, I am coming soon, bringing my recompense, to repay everyone for what he has done."

Ecclesiastes 12:14: "For God will bring every deed into judgment, with every secret thing, whether good or evil."

All of these passages are in complete accord with the Catholic belief that although works themselves do not save us, they are intimately connected with the process of salvation, being always enabled and caused by God's grace. The remarkable thing about these passages is the utter absence of "faith alone" in them. This cannot fail to strike a person who believes in that doctrine (the standard Protestant position).

Why is it that in the very scriptures concerning the final judgment, "faith" is nowhere to be seen, yet mentions of good works are everywhere? It does not seem plausible, given Protestant assumptions. Would the Bible have been written this way if *sola fide* were a true principle and if works — however necessary in the Christian life, as virtually all Christians agree they are — had nothing whatsoever to do with salvation or eternal destiny? I think not.

The desperation of the Protestant position on this particular point (at least on a subscholarly level) was forcefully brought home to me in an Internet dialogue I had on a Protestant discussion board with the professional Calvinist apologist who maintained it. This person believes that Catholicism is apostate, a system of works-righteousness, and no different from "cults" such as those of the Mormons and the Jehovah's Witnesses. His position is that Catholics, therefore, ought to be evangelized, and he makes it clear that this is the purpose for his "Catholicism discussion forum."

This was how he approached me personally. He had no idea whether I was a "saved" Christian (from his perspective) or not. If I were indeed a Christian, it would be, of course, *in spite of* the Catholic Church and its doctrine. This is how millions of Evangelical Protestants think.

So when we first encountered each other, this Calvinist's big question for me was this: if I died that night, and God asked why he should let me enter heaven, what would I say? Would I mention my works, or indulgences, or my prayers to Mary?

I replied that, first of all, I did not see anywhere in the Bible that God ever acts like this (and that I would be happy to be shown otherwise) and that his manner of expression was simply one of many Protestant catch phrases or slogans or evangelistic techniques that cannot be found in the Bible (as far as that goes).

Later, I became curious and proceeded to look up passages concerning judgment, to see what could be learned about how God speaks at those terrible moments of eternal destiny. Sure enough, after I scrutinized the passages above, I discovered that *works* are discussed in *every one* of them, but *never faith*. So I made this point to my Calvinist friend.

I then tried to illustrate for him the shortcomings of the Protestant position in this regard. I stated that if Jesus had attended a good Evangelical seminary and gotten up to speed on his "faith alone" soteriology, his words at the Judgment probably would have been something like the following:

> But when the Son of man comes in his glory, and all the angels with him, then he will sit on his glorious throne. Then he will also say to those on his left, "Depart from me, accursed ones, into the eternal fire which has been prepared for the devil and his angels; for you did not believe in me with faith alone." These will go away into eternal punishment, but the righteous who believed with faith alone into eternal life.

Or:

> Then I saw a great white throne and him who sat upon it, from whose presence earth and heaven fled away, and no place was found for them. And I saw the dead, the great and the small, standing before the throne, and books were opened; and another book was opened, which is the book of life; and the dead were judged from the things which were written in the books, according to whether they had faith alone. And the sea gave up the dead which were in it, and death and Hades gave up the dead which were in them; and

they were judged, every one of them according to whether they had faith alone.

I had some fun with this line of thought, asking rhetorically whether Jesus had attended a liberal synagogue, influenced by heretical "Romish" ideas, and wondering why He kept talking about feeding the hungry, giving water to the thirsty, inviting in strangers, clothing the naked, visiting prisoners, and judging people "according to their deeds"? "What in the world do all these works have to do with salvation?" I asked. Why did Jesus not talk about "faith alone"? Something was seriously wrong.

Biblically speaking, the exact *opposite* of what my Calvinist friend believes is true: if God had asked me his hypothetical question (assuming for the moment that God acts that way), and I replied by recounting the acts of charity and mercy that I had done: feeding the hungry, giving water to the thirsty, inviting in strangers, clothing the naked, visiting prisoners, and various other deeds, I would be listing the reasons for salvation that Jesus himself gave.

Why, then, I asked, did he so disparage the notion that personal works have anything to do with judgment, when the biblical data overwhelmingly indicates that they have *much* to do with it? He could give no answer. My friend had abandoned the discussion on grounds that I was not answering him and that I was muddying the waters and being deliberately evasive. But from my perspective, I was simply inquiring about his premises, and where he was getting his ideas from (and where they did *not* come from), which was altogether relevant to the overall discussion.

To offer an example of scholarly dismissal of the overwhelming evidence of these passages, John Calvin comments on 1 Peter 1:17 in his *Commentaries*:

> By saying, "According to every man's work," he does not refer to merit or to reward; for Peter does not speak here of the

merits of works, nor of the cause of salvation, but he only reminds us that there will be no looking to the person before the tribunal of God, but that what will be regarded will be the real sincerity of the heart. In this place faith also is included in the work.

Calvin uses the same faulty technique we have seen previously, of introducing the element of faith where it is not mentioned, and equating it with works, which *are* mentioned. He also exhibits a common misunderstanding of what Catholics mean by *merit:* as if we were somehow attributing the reward of salvation to man's own self-generated efforts, rather than adopting St. Augustine's maxim that merit is nothing more than offering God's gratuitous, gracious gifts *back* to him.

It is sad that Calvin was continually unaware of how similar in many ways the Catholic position on faith, works, and grace is to his own. His distortions of the Catholic theology of grace (along with Luther's many calumnies and silly statements about Catholicism) have reverberated down through the centuries, causing millions of Protestants to have a warped, deficient view of Catholic teaching, and leading to further unnecessary division.

ST. PAUL: "DOERS OF THE
LAW" WILL BE JUSTIFIED

Romans 2:5-13: "But by your hard and impenitent heart you are storing up wrath for yourself on the day of wrath when God's righteous judgment will be revealed. For he will render to every man according to his works: to those who by patience in well-doing seek for glory and honor and immortality, he will give eternal life; but for those who are factious and do not obey the truth, but obey wickedness, there will be wrath and fury. There will be tribulation and distress for every human being who does evil, the Jew first and also the Greek, but glory and honor and peace for everyone who does good, the Jew first and also the Greek. For God shows no partiality. All who have sinned without the law will also perish without the law, and all who have sinned under the law will be judged by the law. For it is not the hearers of the law who are righteous before God, but the doers of the law who will be justified."

The obvious central place of works in this scenario is similar to the outlook of James, and St. Paul (and that of the Catholic Church). The theme of *obeying the gospel,* or the *obedience of faith,* is common in Paul's writings (e.g., Rom. 1:5, 6:17, 10:16, 15:18-19, 16:25-26; 2 Thess. 1:8; cf. Acts 6:7; Heb. 11:8). Is "faith alone" ever mentioned here? No. Rather, we see works, well-doing, being factious, not obeying, being wicked, doing evil, doing good, sinning, being doers of the law — this is all Paul talks about. Yet Protestants typically tell us, contrary to Jesus, Paul, and James, "We are justified by faith alone, not by faith *and* something we do."

John Calvin, in his commentary on this passage, uses his by-now-familiar technique of contending that when Scripture mentions works, it really means faith and grace, and then proceeds to attack the straw man of supposed Catholic belief in works-righteousness. Amid all that, he seems to assert the biblical and Catholic view that works are man's and God's simultaneously: entirely enabled and caused by God but appropriated by men and made their own; thus justifiably honored by God and having something to do with eternal destiny:

The passages in which it is said that God will reward every man according to his works are easily disposed of.

This is what Protestant commentators often say when a strain of thought in the Bible is *difficult* to dispose of, according to their preconceived systems of theology. Faced with a dilemma, a little display of overconfidence comes in handy.

> For that mode of expression indicates not the cause but the order of sequence.

Nothing whatsoever in the text or context suggests this; Calvin merely *assumes* it. Any assumption may be true or false on other grounds, of course, but something that cannot be located in the text is not exegesis, properly speaking.

> Now, it is beyond doubt that the steps by which the Lord in his mercy consummates our salvation are these, "Whom he did predestinate, them he also called; and whom he called, them he also justified; and whom he justified, them he also glorified" (Rom. 8:30).

Indeed, no one denies that God does these things, but merely asserting these truisms does not overcome the fact that St. Paul places works in a very prominent and "un-Protestant" position here.

> [T]hey are aptly said to work out their own salvation (Phil. 2:12), while by exerting themselves in good works they aspire to eternal life, just as they are elsewhere told to labor for the meat which perisheth not (John 6:27), while they acquire life for themselves by believing in Christ; and yet it is immediately added, that this meat "the Son of man shall give unto you." Hence it appears, that *working* is not at all opposed to *grace*, but refers to pursuit, and, therefore, it follows not that believers are the authors of their own salvation, or that it is the result of their works.

This section is not substantially different from the Catholic position; but Calvin wrongly *thinks* it is, because he mistakenly believes that Catholics accept the notion of works-salvation. The Council of Trent proclaimed the actual Catholic doctrine of salvation and good works:

> [T]he one formal cause [of justification] is the justness of God: not that by which he himself is just, but that by which he makes us just and endowed with which we are renewed in the spirit of our mind, and are not merely considered to be just but we are truly named and are just (Decree on Justification 7).
>
> Jesus Christ himself continually imparts strength to those justified, as the head to the members and the vine to the branches, and this strength always precedes, accompanies and follows their good works, and without it they would be wholly unable to do anything meritorious and pleasing to God (Decree on Justification 16).

Chapter Seven

Baptism

BAPTISM OF ENTIRE HOUSEHOLDS
(IMPLYING THE BAPTISM OF CHILDREN)

Acts 16:15: "And when she was baptized, with her household, she besought us, saying, 'If you have judged me to be faithful to the Lord, come to my house and stay.' And she prevailed upon us" [cf. 18:18].

Acts 16:33: "And he took them the same hour of the night, and washed their wounds, and he was baptized at once, with all his family."

1 Corinthians 1:16: "I did baptize also the household of Stephanas."

Catholics (and other advocates of infant baptism) do not claim that these verses prove that the Bible teaches infant baptism. However, a straightforward reading of them suggests that children were likely baptized along with the household or family of which they were a part. Thus, these verses pose a difficulty for Protestants who oppose infant baptism and must be explained differently.

In Acts 16:15, we read, "She was baptized, with her household." The fact that the verse says *household* rather than simply *husband* is a clear indication of others being involved. Now, who are the members of a household? In that time and culture, it probably would have included parents and maybe grandparents, as well as siblings or cousins. And almost always it would also include children. Extended families are not so common in our culture, but they usually still do (even in our somewhat antilife culture) include children. What's more, many biblical passages connect *household* and *children* (Gen. 18:19, 31:41, 36:6, 47:12; Num. 18:11; 1 Chron. 10:6; Matt. 19:29; 1 Tim. 3:12).

Elsewhere in the Bible, entire households are referred to as being *saved* (Luke 19:9; Acts 11:14, 16:31). To be saved, one does not necessarily have to be aware of what is happening. For example, say a person was born with a severe brain defect and eventually died without ever having been capable of rational thought or communication. Is that person damned simply because of being unable to believe? I think not.

Most Protestants agree with Catholics that God's mercy must extend to those who do not yet know or understand the gospel, or else all aborted babies, children who die at a young age, or before the age of reason, and so forth would go to hell (since they either cannot know or not properly understand the gospel). Therefore, to be saved is not necessarily to understand fully either the gospel or the means of grace by which one is saved (and Catholics, Orthodox, and most Protestants include baptism as a crucial factor in this salvation).

Furthermore, St. Paul in Colossians 2:11-13 makes a connection between baptism and circumcision. Israel was the church before Christ (Acts 7:38; Rom. 9:4). Circumcision, given to boys eight days old, was the seal of the covenant God made with Abraham, which applies to us also (Gal. 3:14, 29). It was a sign of repentance and future faith (Rom. 4:11).

Infants were just as much a part of the covenant as adults (Gen. 17:7; Deut. 29:10-12; cf. Matt. 19:14). Likewise, baptism is the seal of the New Covenant in Christ. It signifies cleansing from sin, just as circumcision did (Deut. 10:16, 30:6; Jer. 4:4, 9:25; Rom. 2:28-9; Phil. 3:3).

John Calvin made these arguments, as did Presbyterian theologian Charles Hodge (1797-1878), and these are some of the reasons Presbyterians and the majority of Protestants throughout history have accepted infant baptism (although they differ on whether it regenerates). But Baptists and others today who believe in adult baptism think that baptism has to be performed after a person has made an informed, educated decision to embrace the gospel of Jesus Christ and be born again. Baptism then serves as a *symbol* of the faith and regeneration, rather than as a *cause* of it. With those presuppositions, infant baptism makes no sense whatsoever, because the infant does not know what is going on, and the knowing is crucial to baptism's purpose, in this conception.

Advocates of this view, then, must explain how these verses pertain to adults but not children. Thus, Augustus Strong (1836-1921), a prominent Baptist theologian, writes about the general issue:

> [T]he passages held to imply infant baptism contain, when fairly interpreted, no reference to such a practice. . . . From Acts 16:15, cf. 40, and Acts 16:33, cf. 34, Neander says that we cannot infer infant baptism. For 1 Cor. 16:15 shows that the whole family of Stephanus, baptized by Paul, were adults (1 Cor. 1:16). It is impossible to suppose a whole heathen household baptized upon the faith of its head (Strong, 951).

But the impossibility resides only in the heads of those who have decided beforehand that the practice is somehow impossible because of prior dogma that does not *permit* it.

Strong argues that the household of Stephanus consisted only of adults, based on 1 Corinthians 16:15, which calls them converts. But the next verse, by very strong implication, refers to them also as men. Does this mean that Stephanus had no wife, or was a widower with children all past the "age of reason" — able to become disciples and to be baptized on their own? Not *necessarily*, for it assumes that the language is all-inclusive when it may not be.

Biblical language is often not as precise and "scientific" as modern language. We know that households *could* certainly include children. And even if we were to grant Strong's contention about this one family, it would not prove at all that *every* such family referred to as being baptized did not have children, or that the children were not also baptized. Nor does even the word *convert* necessarily imply an adult, any more than a "saved" person does (Luke 19:9; Acts 11:14, 16:31).

The biblical case for infant baptism is an argument from plausibility or antecedent probability. The deductions made lead one to conclude that a certain state of affairs is *probable*, more or less, but not absolutely *proven*. These deductive steps with regard to infant baptism are as follows:

1. All agree that the Bible refers to entire households being baptized.

2. It is reasonable to assume that most households (especially in the ancient world) would include children.

3. The Bible specifically places children within the parameters of those persons included in a household (if this commonsense assumption even needs to be asserted), at least eight times (see earlier).

4. Therefore, it is quite likely that baptisms of entire households would include baptisms of children, at least in *some* cases, if not in all.

5. It is quite *unlikely* that baptisms of entire households (granting the premise that the households can and usually do include children) would *never* include children.

6. Therefore, infants (in the greatest likelihood) were baptized.

7. In which case, infant baptism is sanctioned in Scripture, by apostolic example.

A. T. Robertson, a Baptist whom many consider the greatest New Testament Greek scholar of his time, commented on Acts 16:15:

> Who constituted her "household"? The term *oikos*, originally means the building as below, "into my house" and then it includes the inmates of a house. There is nothing here to show whether Lydia's "household" went beyond "the women" employed by her who, like her, had heard the preaching of Paul and had believed. . . . In the household baptisms (Cornelius, Lydia, the jailor, Crispus) one sees "infants" or not according to his predilections or preferences (Robertson, III, 253).

Robertson's last statement is undeniably true, and it harmonizes with what I have always believed about the systematic theological assumptions that we *all* (legitimately, properly) bring to the text, no matter what brand of Christian we are. Thinking itself requires premises and foundational assumptions, and so does biblical exegesis and hermeneutics (interpretation of biblical passages).

Nevertheless, there are stronger probabilities and weaker probabilities. It is a sliding scale. I firmly believe that it is very probable that in this instance, infant baptisms occurred.

Yet I continue to think that if we could make ourselves as "untheological" as humanly possible for a moment, if we could pretend we were from another planet or had never seen a Bible, and look at the two competing cases, we would conclude that the infant-baptism argument is far more plausible. I and those in my camp are certainly not without bias, just as Robertson honestly notes, but in my opinion the logic can hold up on its own.

As for Robertson's argument concerning the makeup of Lydia's household, it may or may not be successful. Reasonable men can certainly differ. I do not find it very persuasive, although it is interesting and has some worth. In any event, it is also based on probability, just as Strong's argument was, and does not rule out other households that were different.

In no way, then, is it decisive for the adult-baptism position. Critics of infant baptism like to point out that the Bible never specifically commands us to baptize infants. But neither does it tell us that we should baptize only adults, or those past the age of reason who can make their own "personal commitment" to Christ.

These kinds of discussions in theology and apologetics are fun and enjoyable (while at the same time serious) precisely because in some areas the biblical evidence is not airtight and involves speculation. As the Christian Church reflected through the centuries, the overwhelming consensus, even among the great majority of Protestants, came to be that infant baptism was God's will, and strongly implied in Holy Scripture.

It *means* something when such consensus has been reached, and we cannot so easily dismiss it. God may communicate his truth to me personally, but he has also done so to millions of other Christians throughout nearly two thousand years. That being the case, views that have garnered "majority support" need at least to be considered respectfully and carefully.

This is not to imply that the majority is always right, but rather, simply to note that Christian tradition is important, allowing for what G. K. Chesterton called "the democracy of the dead."

BAPTISMAL REGENERATION

John 3:5: "Jesus answered, 'Truly, truly, I say to you, unless one is born of water and the Spirit, he cannot enter the kingdom of God.' "

Acts 2:38: "And Peter said to them, 'Repent, and be baptized every one of you in the name of Jesus Christ for the forgiveness of your sins; and you shall receive the gift of the Holy Spirit.' "

Acts 22:16: " 'And now why do you wait? Rise and be baptized, and wash away your sins, calling on his name.' "

1 Corinthians 6:11: "And such were some of you. But you were washed, you were sanctified, you were justified in the name of the Lord Jesus Christ and in the Spirit of our God."

Titus 3:5: "He saved us, not because of deeds done by us in righteousness, but in virtue of his own mercy, by the washing of regeneration and renewal in the Holy Spirit."

1 Peter 3:19-21: ". . . in which he went and preached to the spirits in prison, who formerly did not obey, when God's patience waited in the days of Noah, during the building of the ark, in which a few, that is, eight persons, were saved through water. Baptism, which corresponds to this, now saves you, not as a removal of dirt from the body but as an appeal to God for a clear conscience, through the resurrection of Jesus Christ."

Baptismal regeneration is understood by Catholics (and Orthodox, Lutherans, traditional Anglicans, Methodists, and some other Protestants, in a basic agreement) to mean a spiritual rebirth. Just as a human being must be physically generated to enter the world, he must be spiritually regenerated to enter the kingdom of heaven. The passages above constitute the major scriptural reasons why the great majority of Christians for two thousand years have accepted this belief, and accept baptism as a sacrament: a physical means to convey God's grace.

Protestants who deny baptismal regeneration (Baptists, Presbyterians, many Pentecostals, and others) place spiritual regeneration at the point of personal conversion or a decision to become a disciple of Jesus. Some still practice infant baptism, but deny that it regenerates. Most groups that practice only adult baptism deny that it regenerates, but some (such as the Church of Christ) believe in an adult ("believer's") baptism that also regenerates. The passages presently under consideration make the "non-regeneration" position difficult to accept, since they associate baptism directly with salvation.

Even Martin Luther substantially agrees with the position of the Catholic Church:

> Little children . . . are free in every way, secure and saved solely through the glory of their baptism. . . . Through the prayer of the believing church which presents it . . . the infant is changed, cleansed, and renewed by inpoured faith (*The Babylonian Captivity of the Church*, 1520, in Steinhauser, 197).

> [E]xpressed in the simplest form, the power, the effect, the benefit, the fruit, and the purpose of baptism is to save. . . . [T]hrough the Word, baptism receives the power to become the washing of regeneration, as St. Paul calls it in Titus 3:5. . . . [F]aith clings to the water and believes it to be baptism which effects pure salvation and life (*Large Catechism*, 1529, sects. 223-224, p. 162).

John Calvin, on the other hand, takes a view much more similar to the majority of Evangelical Protestants today. He wrote, concerning John 3:5:

> By "water and the Spirit" . . . I simply understand the Spirit, which is water. . . . [T]o be born again of water, and of the Spirit, is nothing else than to receive that power of the

Spirit, which has the same effect on the soul that water has on the body (*Institutes*, IV, 16, 25).

This verse is not self-interpreting, and one must bring some assumptions to it. So Calvin makes the water metaphorical; others take it literally as the water of baptism. In such cases, it is good to compare Scripture with Scripture and determine whether there are any obvious parallels, to help determine what the less-clear passages might mean. We might compare, for example, Titus 3:5 with John 3:5:

> **Titus 3:5:** "[H]e saved us, not because of deeds done by us in righteousness, but in virtue of his own mercy, by the washing of regeneration and renewal in the Holy Spirit."

> **John 3:5:** "Jesus answered, 'Truly, truly, I say to you, unless one is born of water and the Spirit, he cannot enter the kingdom of God.' "

The two passages are almost exactly parallel:

Titus	John
Saved	Enter the kingdom of God
Washing of regeneration	Born of water
Renewal in the Holy Spirit	Born of . . . the Spirit

What is "washing" in one verse (with two other common elements) is "water" in the other. Thus, baptism is tied to salvation, in accord with the other verses above. 1 Corinthians 6:11 is also similar to Titus 3:5 and John 3:5: "And such were some of you. But you were washed, you were sanctified, you were justified in the name of the Lord Jesus Christ and in the Spirit of our God."

The "justified" is the parallel of "kingdom of God" and "saved" in Titus 3:5 and John 3:5; "washed" goes along with "washing of regeneration" and "born of water," and all this was done by the

Spirit. Now, it is a striking *threefold* parallelism. Furthermore, it is notable that baptism, justification, and sanctification are all mentioned together. This cross-referencing supports the argument that both baptism and regeneration are the subject matter of John 3:5. I shall also answer Calvin with Luther:

> Christ says clearly and concisely that the birth referred to here must take place through water and the Holy Spirit. This new birth is Baptism. . . . And begone with everyone who refuses to accept this doctrine!
>
> . . . [W]e reply, "Of course, they believed that John purified by his Baptism; for by means of it he joined you to Christ." Thus one is saved according to the way in which Christ instructed Nicodemus (John 3:5) (*Sermons on the Gospel of St. John*, chs. 1-4, 1540; in LW, 22, 287-288, 429).

The analogy to John the Baptist's baptism is interesting and affords us more biblical parallels to John 3:5. For John, baptism was the way to the kingdom of heaven ("a baptism of repentance for the forgiveness of sins": Mark 1:4). Christian baptism likewise forgives sins, because it regenerates. Why should an ordinary Christian baptism have less power than John's, and not be able to wipe away sins as his did?

When Jesus arrived to begin his mission, the first thing he did was to be baptized by John (Mark 1:9), as an example (of course, he technically did not *need* to repent or be baptized). And what happened when Jesus was baptized? The Holy Spirit descended upon him (Mark 1:10). Thus, the Holy Spirit is present *alongside* the water of baptism, but is not identical to the water, as in Calvin's view of John 3:5.

Also, we see that the water *preceded* the Spirit, rather than vice versa, as in Calvin's view. Cross-referencing, then, makes the baptism (and regenerational) interpretation of John 3:5 much more plausible.

How, then, does Calvin interpret Titus 3:5? He plays word games and engages in blatant eisegesis regarding that passage and also 1 Peter 3:21:

> The first object, therefore, for which it is appointed by the Lord, is to be a sign and evidence of our purification, or (better to explain my meaning) it is a kind of sealed instrument. . . . [W]e are to receive it in connection with the promise, "He that believeth and is baptized shall be saved" (Mark 16:16).
>
> Peter also says that "baptism also doth now save us" (1 Pet. 3:21). For he did not mean to intimate that our ablution and salvation are perfected by water, or that water possesses in itself the virtue of purifying, regenerating, and renewing; nor does he mean that it is the cause of salvation, but only that the knowledge and certainty of such gifts are perceived in this sacrament (*Institutes*, IV, 15, 1-2).

Whereas in dealing with John 3:5, Calvin allegorized the water, here he interprets the "washing" of Titus 3:5 as indeed referring to baptism (cf. *Institutes*, IV, 15, 5 — which only strengthens the analogies made above), but then he proceeds arbitrarily to change the *function* of baptism in relation to regeneration, claiming it merely *follows* the latter (as a sign of something already accomplished on other grounds) and does not *cause* it.

This theory is neat and tidy, but can it be deduced from the biblical text? If we examine just the texts mentioned in this section, Calvin's conclusion simply does not follow. It is a forced, strained interpretation. The text of Titus reads, "He saved us . . . by the washing of regeneration." For Calvin's theory to work, the Revised Calvin Version (RCV) would have to read, "The washing of regeneration is a sign and seal that he has saved us." The two thoughts are completely different. Calvin's logic is as absurd as the following analogy, based on the sentence structure and logic of Titus 3:5:

Text: He saved me by the throwing of a life jacket.

Interpretation: But one cannot be saved by the throwing of a life jacket, because a life jacket is only a sign and symbol that one has been saved. One is already saved from drowning, and then the life jacket is thrown out to show the world that the rescuing has already occurred.

This makes no sense whatsoever. The text clearly states a particular application of the general proposition "X was caused by Y" (or, "Y caused X" — which is the same logical proposition). The chain of causation flows from Y (baptism) to X (salvation); one cannot simply deny this (if words have any meaning); the logic and the grammatical structure of the sentence do not allow it. Calvin might better have stuck to his method of making water or washing strictly metaphorical. Once he admitted that these verses do indeed refer to baptism, he predestined himself to logical confusion and exegetical chaos.

1 Peter 3:21 could not be any clearer than it is: "Baptism . . . now saves you." The RCV (applying Calvin's exegesis) would have to read, "Baptism now gives you the knowledge and certainty of salvation." Again, this is as logically foolish as believing that the following two sentences express the same idea:

Doctor: Heart surgery will now save your life.

New Age Psychologist: Heart surgery won't save your life, but will give you the knowledge and certainty that your life is saved.

Calvin tries to explain away the baptismal regeneration of 1 Peter 3:21 by overemphasizing the "clear conscience" that Peter also mentions (see *Institutes*, IV, 14, 24). But I think context is decisive in upholding the Catholic interpretation of 1 Peter 3:21. We see that by adding verses 19 and 20 (as above).

The meaning is much clearer in context. This is a typical Hebraic parallelism, or what is called "types and shadows," very common in Scripture. In the Old Testament, when salvation was mentioned, it usually referred to winning a battle, being saved from an enemy, having one's life or town saved, and so forth — in other words, physical salvation. This became a metaphor for spiritual salvation later on, in New Testament thought. Here, Peter makes the same sort of analogy. The eight persons in Noah's ark were *saved through water*, i.e., physically saved from drowning. The water of the flood symbolized baptism that *now saves you* also, spiritually, from sin.

As Noah and his family were saved through water, so Christians are saved by baptism, not merely "symbolically saved," or "doing a necessary but not salvific ritual after being saved, to show forth a sign and seal of our salvation," which makes no sense of the passage and twists the parallelism itself.

Calvin plays similar games with Acts 22:16, pretending that God cannot use matter to convey his grace — that this somehow detracts from the sole sufficiency of the blood of Christ and his atonement. In other words, he denies the sacramental principle shown repeatedly in Scripture.

But he is again operating from his own preconceived notions and false dichotomies, not from the *biblical data*. When people like Catholics and Lutherans and Orthodox *do* accept the biblical evidence for baptismal regeneration in its plain meaning, Calvin treats them in the following fashion, in his comment on this verse:

> It is well known how much the Papists differ from this rule, who tie the cause of grace to their exorcisms and enchantments; and they are so far from studying to direct the miserable people unto Christ, that they rather drown Christ in baptism, and pollute his sacred name by their enchantments.

Martin Luther (I remind Protestant readers) would also be included in this "anathema," since he holds an even stronger view than the Catholic one: in his view, the grace of baptism cannot be lost:

Thus the papists have attacked our position and declared that anyone who falls into sin after his Baptism must undergo a distinct type of purification (*Sermons on the Gospel of St. John*, chs. 1-4, 1540; in LW, 22, 429-430).

John Wesley, the founder of Methodism, but actually a lifelong Anglican (reasoning much like St. Augustine often does), accepts the notion of baptism's being a seal, without denying that it is at the same time a means or cause of regeneration. He does not dichotomize as Calvin does, but thinks in far more biblically oriented terms. Hence, he comments in his *Notes on the New Testament*, on John 3:5, Acts 22:16, Titus 3:5, and 1 Peter 3:21:

Except a man be born of water and of the Spirit — except he experience that great inward change by the Spirit, and be baptized (wherever baptism can be had) as the outward sign and means of it.

Baptism administered to real penitents is both a means and seal of pardon. Nor did God ordinarily in the primitive Church bestow this on any, unless through this means.

Sanctification, expressed by the laver of regeneration (that is, baptism, the thing signified, as well as the outward sign). . . .

[T]hrough the water of baptism we are saved from the sin which overwhelms the world as a flood: not, indeed, the bare outward sign, but the inward grace. . . .

Elsewhere Wesley makes this even clearer:

[T]here is a justification conveyed to us in our baptism, or, properly, this state is then begun (*The Principles of a Methodist Farther Explained*, 1746; in Lindstrom, 106-107).

So we see that several groups of Protestants accept a view of baptism virtually identical or quite similar to the Catholic one:

that baptism effects spiritual regeneration in a person; it is a means, not a sign, of justification. Naturally, we think their exegesis and biblical support is that much better, but readers can draw their own conclusions.

Chapter Eight

The Eucharist

THE LAST SUPPER: "THIS IS MY BODY"

Luke 22:19-20: "And he took bread, and when he had given thanks he broke it and gave it to them, saying, 'This is my body which is given for you. Do this in remembrance of me.' And likewise the cup after supper, saying, 'This cup which is poured out for you is the new covenant in my blood.' "

The Catholic Church teaches the Real Presence of Christ in the Holy Eucharist (or, Holy Communion, or the Lord's Supper, as Protestants often refer to it). By *Real Presence*, Catholics mean that Jesus Christ is actually and substantially present (not just subjectively or symbolically) after the bread and wine are consecrated and truly become the Body and Blood of Jesus. By *transubstantiation* (literally, "change of substance"), we mean that the bread and wine completely change into the Body and Blood of Jesus. The substance changes, but the outward properties, or accidents, remain the same. It is a mystery and must be believed by faith.

The controversy over the nature of the Eucharist has always been an important one in Protestant-Catholic history, because it touches upon what Catholics, Orthodox, and some Protestants consider the central rite of Christian worship. Therefore, it is important to survey the biblical teaching thoroughly and try to arrive at some conclusions.

Martin Luther's eucharistic theology was much closer to Catholic than to Calvinist or Reformed theology (or the purely symbolic conception, which took it a step further). Luther believed in the Real Presence, although he denied transubstantiation and rejected the Sacrifice of the Mass. According to his nominalistic, anti-Scholastic leanings, he did not want to speculate about metaphysics and how the bread and wine became the Body and Blood of Christ. He simply believed in the miracle of the literal presence of Jesus' Body and Blood "alongside" the bread and wine (*consubstantiation*). In this respect, his position was similar to the Eastern Orthodox one.

> It is enough for me that Christ's blood is present; let it be with the wine as God wills. Before I would drink mere wine with the Enthusiasts, I would rather have pure blood with the Pope (early 1520s; in Althaus, 376; LW, 37, 317).
>
> The glory of our God is precisely that for our sakes he comes down to the very depths, into human flesh, into the bread, into our mouth, our heart, our body (in Althaus, 398; LW, 37, 71 ff.).

In the Last Supper passages (Luke 22:19-20; cf. Matt. 26:26-28, Mark 14:22-24), nothing in the actual text supports a metaphorical interpretation. Elsewhere in Scripture, where the word is meant to be figurative, it is readily apparent (Matt. 13:38; John 10:7, 15:1; 1 Cor. 10:4), whereas here it is not. The Last Supper was the Jewish feast of Passover, which involved eating a sacrificial lamb. The disciples could hardly have missed the significance of what Jesus was saying. Before and after this passage, he spoke of his imminent suffering (Luke 22:15-16, 18, 21-22). John the Baptist had already referred to him as the Lamb of God (John 1:29).

Protestantism's founders vary in their interpretation of this verse and in their eucharistic theology. John Calvin's "mystical" view of the Eucharist is complex and not quickly summarized or refuted. Ulrich Zwingli (the Protestant "Reformer" of Zurich) held to a symbolic view, on the other hand, which seems to have prevailed among many Evangelical Protestants today. We shall concentrate on the exegetical and logical weakness of Zwingli's arguments in this chapter. He wrote about this passage:

> In the words: "This is my body," the word *this* means the bread, and the word *body*, the body which is put to death for us. Therefore the word *is* cannot be taken literally, for the bread is not the body and cannot be. . . . "This is my body" means, "The bread signifies my body" or "is a figure of my body" (*On the Lord's Supper*, 1526; in Bromiley, 225).

Yet Martin Luther refutes this line of thinking, using the very same scriptures:

> [T]his word of Luke and Paul is clearer than sunlight and more overpowering than thunder. First, no one can deny that he speaks of the cup, since he says, "This is the cup." Secondly, he calls it the cup of the new testament. This is overwhelming, for it could not be a new testament by means and on account of wine alone (*Against the Heavenly Prophets in the Matter of Images and Sacraments*, 1525; LW, 40, 217).

In that same work, Luther makes a fascinating argument that a purely symbolic Eucharist turns the sacrament into a futile work of man rather than a grace and blessing from God:

> He thinks one does not see that out of the word of Christ he makes a pure commandment and law which accomplishes nothing more than to tell and bid us to remember

and acknowledge him. Furthermore, he makes this acknowledgment nothing else than a work that we do, while we receive nothing else than bread and wine (*Against the Heavenly Prophets in the Matter of Images and Sacraments*, 1525; LW, 40, 206).

Martin Luther rebukes the symbolic view of the Eucharist, held by most Evangelicals today:

[S]ince we are confronted by God's words, "This is my body" — distinct, clear, common, definite words, which certainly are no trope, either in Scripture or in any language — we must embrace them with faith. . . . [N]ot as hairsplitting sophistry dictates but as God says them for us, we must repeat these words after him and hold to them (*Confession Concerning Christ's Supper*, 1528; in Althaus, 390).

The next passage we shall consider, John 6, offers even more compelling proof than the preceding one and is a source of perpetual controversy among Christians.

"HE WHO EATS MY FLESH AND DRINKS MY BLOOD HAS ETERNAL LIFE"

John 6:47-66: " 'Truly, truly, I say to you, he who believes has eternal life. I am the bread of life. Your fathers ate the manna in the wilderness, and they died. This is the bread which comes down from heaven, that a man may eat of it and not die. I am the living bread which came down from heaven; if anyone eats of this bread, he will live forever; and the bread which I shall give for the life of the world is my flesh.' The Jews then disputed among themselves, saying, 'How can this man give us his flesh to eat?' So Jesus said to them, 'Truly, truly, I say to you, unless you eat the flesh of the Son of man and drink his blood, you have no life in you; he who eats my flesh and drinks my blood has eternal life, and I will raise him up at the last day. For my flesh is food indeed, and my blood is drink indeed. He who eats my flesh and drinks my blood abides in me, and I in him. As the living Father sent me, and I live because of the Father, so he who eats me will live because of me. This is the bread which came down from heaven, not such as the fathers ate and died; he who eats this bread will live forever.'

"This he said in the synagogue, as he taught at Capernaum. Many of his disciples, when they heard it, said, 'This is a hard saying; who can listen to it?' But Jesus, knowing in himself that his disciples murmured at it, said to them, 'Do you take offense at this? Then what if you were to see the Son of man ascending where he was before? It is the spirit that gives life, the flesh is of no avail; the words that I have spoken to you are spirit and life. But there are some of you that do not believe.' For Jesus knew from the first who those were that did not believe, and who it was that would betray him. And he said, 'This is why I told you that no one can come to me unless it is granted him by the Father.' After this many of his disciples drew back and no longer went about with him."

The Catholic interpretation of this passage may be described briefly as follows: with regard to John 6 and Jesus' repeatedly commanding the hearers to "eat my flesh and drink my blood," it is known that in the Jewish culture of that time, metaphors such as this were used to signify doing someone grievous injury (see, e.g.,

Job 19:22; Ps. 27:2; Eccles. 4:5; Isa. 9:20, 49:26; Mic. 3:1-3; Rev. 16:6).

Therefore, it is not plausible to assert that Jesus was speaking metaphorically, according to the standard Protestant hermeneutic of interpreting Scripture in light of contemporary usages, customs, and idioms.

As Luther points out below, when the words *flesh* and *spirit* are opposed to each other in the New Testament, it is always a figurative use, in the sense of sinful human nature (flesh) contrasted with humanity enriched by God's grace (spirit). This can be clearly seen in passages such as Matthew 26:41; Romans 7:5-6, 25, 8:1-14; 1 Corinthians 5:5; 2 Corinthians 7:1; Galatians 3:3, 4:29, 5:13-26; and 1 Peter 3:18, 4:6.

Many Protestants today assert that this passage has symbolic meaning only; metaphor is often used in Scripture, and this seems to be another instance of that. Zwingli offers us an example of early Protestant "symbolist" reasoning:

> There can be no doubt that only the spirit can give life to the soul. For how could the physical flesh either nourish or give life to the soul?
>
> [W]ith his own words Christ teaches us that everything which he says concerning the eating of flesh or bread has to be understood in terms of believing. . . . [T]his passage tells us that the carnal eating of Christ's flesh and blood profiteth nothing, and you have introduced such a carnal eating into the sacrament (*On the Lord's Supper*, 1526; in Bromiley, 206-207, 210-211).

Martin Luther expounded the text otherwise. Preaching on John 6, he stated:

> All right! There we have it! This is clear, plain, and unconcealed: "I am speaking of my flesh and blood."

. . . There we have the flat statement which cannot be interpreted in any other way than that there is no life, but death alone, apart from His flesh and blood if these are neglected or despised. How is it possible to distort this text? . . . You must note these words and this text with the utmost diligence. . . . It can neither speciously be interpreted nor avoided and evaded (*Sermons on the Gospel of St. John: Chapters 6-8,* 1532; LW, 23, 133-135).

Luther's eucharistic theology was not identical to Catholic theology, but it was far closer to it than to the symbolic view. Luther thought that Jesus' Body and Blood were present "alongside" the bread and wine after consecration. So Jesus was really there, but the bread and wine were there, too — a phenomenon called "consubstantiation" — whereas in the Catholic theology of transubstantiation, they cease to be bread and wine after consecration.

Many Protestants argue that Jesus was not referring to the Eucharist at all in John 6, but merely to belief in Him, expressed in symbolic terms. The word *Eucharist* comes from the Greek words *eucharistia, eucharisteo,* and *eucharistos.* Together these occur fifty-four times in the New Testament, so obviously *Eucharist* is an eminently biblical word. Its meaning is "thanks," "thankfulness," or "thanksgiving."

But how is that related to the Last Supper, or the Lord's Supper, or Holy Communion? It's very simple:

> **Matthew 26:27-28:** "And he took a cup, and when he had given *thanks,* he gave it to them, saying, 'Drink of it, all of you; for this is my blood of the covenant' " (cf. Mark 14:23; Luke 22:17, 19).

There is a fascinating parallel between this language and that used in the feeding of the four thousand and the five thousand. Scripture records that Jesus "gave thanks" on those occasions, and then "broke" the fish and the loaves and "gave them to the disciples, and the disciples gave them to the crowds" (Matt. 15:36; cf. Mark 8:6). Likewise, we see the same progression in the accounts of the Last Supper:

> **Luke 22:19:** "And he took bread, and when he had given *thanks*, he broke it, and gave it to them, saying, 'This is my body which is given for you. Do this in remembrance of me' " (cf. Matt. 26:26; 1 Cor. 10:16, 11:23-24; Acts 2:42, 20:7).

So we have already established a parallel between the Last Supper and the ritual initiated by Jesus there (which is the central essence of the Mass), and the miraculous feeding of the crowds with bread and fish. In John 6, the same miracle occurs, except that this time the biblical writer records that Jesus ties the two together explicitly. First, we have the narrative concerning the feeding:

> **John 6:11:** "Jesus then took the loaves, and when he had given *thanks [eucharisteo]*, he distributed them to those who were seated" (cf. 6:23).

John 6:22 informs us that the rest of the story took place on the following day. But Jesus had a rebuke for the people who sought him out on this occasion:

> **John 6:26-27:** " '[Y]ou seek me, not because you saw signs, but because you ate your fill of the loaves. Do not labor for the food which perishes, but for the food which endures to eternal life, which the Son of man will give to you.' "

In other words, Jesus is contrasting the utility of physical food with eucharistic, sacramental food (his own Body). He continues, getting more and more explicit as he goes along:

John 6:35: " 'I am the bread of life; he who comes to me shall not hunger' " (cf. 6:33).

John 6:51: " 'I am the living bread which came down from heaven; if anyone eats of this bread, he will live forever; and the bread which I shall give for the life of the world is my flesh' " (cf. 6:48-50).

John continues:

John 6:52: "The Jews then disputed among themselves, saying, 'How can this man give us his flesh to eat?' "

Does Jesus then say, "Look, guys, settle down; you misunderstood me! I was just talking symbolically. Don't be so literal"? No, not at all. Rather, he reiterates his point in the strongest, most literal language (John 6:53-58).

When Jesus told parables, he always explained them, lest their meaning be lost on the hearers (and us readers of the Bible). When his hearers did not understand what he was saying, he always explained it more fully (e.g., Matt. 19:24-26; John 11:11-14, 8:32-34; cf. 4:31-34, 8:21-23).

But when they *refused* to accept some teaching, Jesus merely repeated it with more emphasis (e.g., Matt. 9:2-7; John 8:56-58). That is what he does here, even though many of these people abandoned him as a result of his difficult teaching (6:60-61, 64, 66-67). By analogy, then, we conclude that John 6 was an instance of willful rejection (see John 6:63-65; cf. Matt. 13:10-23).

I think it is quite obvious that Jesus is referring to the Eucharist (and the Real Presence) in John 6, for these reasons:

1. The parallelism between the miraculous mass feedings and the Last Supper.

2. The use of *eucharisteo* in the descriptions of both instances, in the same fashion.

3. Christ's repeated reference in John 6 to his Body (i.e., eucharistically; sacramentally) giving eternal life to the recipients (John 6:27, 33, 50-51, 54, 58). This is clearly not merely referring to belief in him; if that were the case, explicit references to his Body and Blood would be entirely superfluous. He could have just spoken in terms of belief rather than of eating and drinking his Flesh and Blood (which he did in many other instances, e.g., John 12:44-46; 14:10-12).

4. The equation of (what appeared to be) bread and his Body in John 6 and the Last Supper (Matt. 26:26; Mark 14:22; Luke 22:19; 1 Cor. 10:16-17, 11:23-24, 27, 29; John 6:33, 48, 50-51, 53-58).

5. The equation of (what appeared to be) wine and his Blood in both John 6 and the Last Supper (Matt. 26:27-28; Mark 14:23-24; Luke 22:20; 1 Cor. 10:16, 11:25, 27; John 6:53-56).

We conclude, then, that all indications in John 6 point to a Real Presence, and not mere symbolism. The "realist" view alone consistently incorporates and explains cross-exegesis and the meanings of the words used.

"PARTICIPATION" IN THE
BODY AND BLOOD OF CHRIST

> **1 Corinthians 10:16:** "The cup of blessing which we bless, is it not a participation in the blood of Christ? The bread which we break, is it not a participation in the body of Christ?"

This verse again allows us to observe, in a nutshell, traditional Protestant controversies in their own ranks. Catholics interpret it literally, but Protestants differ among themselves. Zwingli special pleads in his interpretation of the passage:

> [W]hen you offer thanks with the cup and the bread, eating and drinking together, you signify thereby that you are one

body and one bread, namely, the body which is the Church of Christ" (*On the Lord's Supper*, 1526; in Bromiley, 237).

But Martin Luther again refutes this specious interpretation and offers us a unique insight into a Protestant exegete who had every motivation to disagree with the Catholic Church's interpretation, but in the end was forced by the text to accept its straightforward meaning:

> I confess that if Karlstadt, or anyone else, could have convinced me five years ago that only bread and wine were in the sacrament, he would have done me a great service. At that time I suffered such severe conflicts and inner strife and torment that I would gladly have been delivered from them. I realized that at this point I could best resist the papacy. . . . But I am a captive and cannot free myself. The text is too powerfully present, and will not allow itself to be torn from its meaning by mere verbiage (*Letter to the Christians at Strassburg in Opposition to the Fanatic Spirit*, 1524; LW, 68).

For Luther, the passage is quite compelling:

> Even if we had no other passage than this, we could sufficiently strengthen all consciences and sufficiently overcome all adversaries. . . . He could not have spoken more clearly and strongly (*Against the Heavenly Prophets in the Matter of Images and Sacraments*, 1525; LW, 40, 177, 181).

Luther thinks the realist, concrete, nonsymbolic nature of the verse is obvious, to the point where he seems to be irritated (the three-time repetition of "it is") that others cannot see what is so clear:

> The bread which is broken or distributed piece by piece is the participation in the body of Christ. It is, it is, it is, he

says, the participation in the body of Christ. Wherein does the participation in the body of Christ consist? It cannot be anything else than that as each takes a part of the broken bread he takes therewith the body of Christ (*Against the Heavenly Prophets in the Matter of Images and Sacraments*, 1525; LW, 40, 178).

PROFANING THE BODY AND BLOOD OF THE LORD

1 Corinthians 11:27-30: "Whoever, therefore, eats the bread or drinks the cup of the Lord in an unworthy manner will be guilty of profaning the body and blood of the Lord. Let a man examine himself, and so eat of the bread and drink of the cup. For anyone who eats and drinks without discerning the body eats and drinks judgment upon himself. That is why many of you are weak and ill, and some have died."

St. Paul hints at the sacredness of the Eucharist when he warns (using extremely strong language) of the consequences of receiving it without reverence and discernment. The implication is quite clear: something more than mere bread and wine, more than a pleasant "memorial meal," is going on here.

But again, many Protestants today have lost the sacramental outlook of Martin Luther (and to a lesser extent, even of John Calvin). Baptist apologist James White provides a contemporary version of Zwinglian symbolism:

Participation in the Supper is meant to be a memorial (not a sacrifice) of the death of Christ, not the carefree and impious party it had become at Corinth (White, 175).

Martin Luther would have a great problem with such reasoning, and in refuting it, he closely approximates what a Catholic response would be. He argues that it is pointless for St. Paul to speak of sin here ("profaning" in the text) if Jesus "is not present in the eating of the bread" and that "the nature and character of the sentence requires" this "clear" interpretation. Luther sums up his exegetical argument:

> It is not sound reasoning arbitrarily to associate the sin which St. Paul attributes to eating with remembrance of Christ, of which Paul does not speak. For he does not say, "Who unworthily holds the Lord in remembrance," but "Who unworthily eats and drinks" (*Against the Heavenly Prophets in the Matter of Images and Sacraments*, 1525; LW, 40, 183-184).

I prefer what is often called the "superstition" of Martin Luther, St. Augustine, and the Fathers of the Church, as it seems to be far and away the most natural reading of all these texts. Augustine wrote:

> [I]t is the Body of the Lord and the Blood of the Lord even in those to whom the Apostle said: "Whoever eats and drinks unworthily, eats and drinks judgment to himself" (Baptism, 5, 8, 9; in Jurgens, III, 68).

The eucharistic "Catholic verses" are some of the most important in the entire Catholic exegetical and apologetic arsenal. In order to avoid their clear meaning, Protestants must skirt them, special plead, and read their own prior biases into texts. This is, of course, all contrary to the usual Protestant acknowledgment that Scripture is to be interpreted literally unless the text clearly indicates otherwise.

These passages are so compelling that they played a crucial role in producing a nearly unanimous patristic acceptance of the Real Presence in the Eucharist. Several major Protestant Church historians and experts on history of Christian doctrine note this (e.g.,

Otto W. Heick, Williston Walker, Philip Schaff, Jaroslav Pelikan, and Carl Volz). The historical facts on this point are indisputable. As just one representative statement, I cite J.N.D. Kelly, perhaps the most-cited patristics scholar:

> One could multiply texts like these which show Augustine taking for granted the traditional identification of the elements with the sacred body and blood. There can be no doubt that he shared the realism held by almost all of his contemporaries and predecessors (Kelly, 447).

Catholics need not be shy in defending the Real Presence of Christ in the Eucharist. The biblical evidence is very strong, and so is the history of the beliefs of the early Christians on this score. We have nothing to fear, and we can decisively win this battle of "competing eucharistic theologies" on the field of Scripture and history alike.

Chapter Nine

Penance

SHARING IN CHRIST'S SUFFERINGS

Philippians 3:10: ". . . that I may know him and the power of his resurrection, and may share his sufferings, becoming like him in his death" (cf. Gal. 2:20).

Romans 8:17: ". . . and if children, then heirs, heirs of God and fellow heirs with Christ, provided we suffer with him in order that we may also be glorified with him" (cf. 1 Cor. 15:31; 2 Cor. 6:9; 1 Pet. 4:1, 13).

These passages illustrate the central place of suffering in the Christian life. In Romans 8:17 this motif comes right in the midst of a Pauline teaching widely considered by Protestants to be a joyful, "triumphal" exhortation. The biblical worldview incorporates suffering and joy side by side. They are not seen as incompatible or contradictory. I once wrote, humorously and tongue-in-cheek (but with a very serious point to make), about Romans 8:17 in one of my Internet dialogues:

How quickly we forget the book of Job and all of St. Paul's intense sufferings (and he says to "imitate" him). Even in the glorious, fabulous passage of Romans 8, where Paul is all excited about the Holy Spirit and how he helps us overcome all obstacles, what does he also say? He is going along, talking like a good "born again," sanctified, set-free, "filled with the Holy Ghost" Evangelical Protestant, and then suddenly (unless one ignores this part, as I did in my Protestant days) he becomes a morbid, masochistic, crucifix-clutching Catholic and takes away everyone's fun and peaches and cream: ". . . if children, then heirs, heirs of God and fellow heirs with Christ, *provided we suffer* with him *in order* that we may also be glorified with him."

Boo! Get a life, Paul! What a party pooper Paul is. Why can't he lighten up and accept what Jesus has for him? How did he become so "Catholic"? What a drag. Someone needs to straighten him out quickly as to what the victorious Christian life is all about.

There is no need to consult commentaries at this point, for our purposes. They will not deny that a Christian needs to, and can *expect* to, suffer. It is only certain strains of Evangelical Protestantism (particularly one brand of Pentecostal, "name it, claim it" Protestantism, which asserts that believers can have whatever they like merely by having enough faith to "claim" it) that try to pretend that suffering is foreign to the Christian life (in extreme cases, it is not God's will *at all* that we even have sickness, and so forth), who ignore this crucial aspect of the passage. They pass right over it as if it were not even there.

Most Evangelicals do not take it that far, yet still minimize the place of suffering, and hence, of the related notion, penance. This represents a scandalous lack of understanding of the deeper, more difficult aspects of Christianity.

My emphasis here is simply that such suffering is directly tied to the *spiritual benefits* of a Christian, derived from Christ, and that this aspect or factor cannot be underestimated. In Romans 8:17 it is very clear: *unless* we suffer, we cannot be glorified with Christ (no reward without the sweat and the toil).

This suffering is viewed by Catholics as a certain wholly secondary participation in the Atonement, in the sense that it can be applied to help others (solely because of the empowerment obtained by our Lord Jesus on the Cross), just as our prayers can, and that this was God's design and plan.

This doctrine and perspective gives the highest meaning to suffering: it can be helpful and beneficial to others, just as Jesus' and Paul's sufferings were. It is no longer meaningless, but can lead to a greater good. St. Paul wrote, for example, in Philippians 2:17, "I am to be poured out as a libation upon the sacrificial offering of your faith" (cf. 2 Cor 6:4-10).

This is very "unevangelical" language (so passages like these are rarely discussed in nonscholarly Evangelical Protestant circles), but quite harmonious with Catholic theology and spirituality.

CARRYING CHRIST'S AFFLICTIONS IN OUR BODIES

2 Corinthians 4:10: ". . . always carrying in the body the death of Jesus, so that the life of Jesus may also be manifested in our bodies" (cf. 1:5-7; Gal. 6:17; 2 Tim. 4:6).

Colossians 1:24: "Now I rejoice in my sufferings for your sake, and in my flesh I complete what is lacking in Christ's afflictions for the sake of his body, that is, the church" (cf. Rom. 12:1; 2 Cor. 11:23-30).

Catholics hold, with Protestants, that Jesus' Passion was complete and infinite in atoning power. The Council of Trent made this very clear, in its treatment of penance (Chapter 8: "On the Necessity and on the Fruit of Satisfaction"):

> For we who can do nothing of ourselves, as of ourselves, can do all things, He cooperating who strengthens us (Phil. 4:13). Thus, man has not wherein to glory, but all our glorying is in Christ (1 Cor. 1:31; 2 Cor. 10:17; Gal. 6:14).

God allows us to take part in the great drama of redemption by allowing us to share the sufferings of Christ that brought it about. That does not mean that the cause of redemption does not completely lie with Jesus Christ, but that we can be *part* of it in some mysterious way (in his will and by his design and providence), just as our prayers are part of his redemption and our works are part of salvation (1 Cor. 3:8-9, 15:10; Eph. 2:8-10; Phil. 2:12-13) — although everything, of course, goes back to God as Sovereign and First Cause.

John Calvin (as a representative Protestant) makes a scathing criticism of the Catholic exegesis of Colossians 1:24, claiming that it detracts from the finished work of Christ:

> Indeed, as their whole doctrine is a patchwork of sacrilege and blasphemy, this is the most blasphemous of the whole. . . . What is this but merely to leave the name of Christ, and at the same time make him a vulgar saintling, who can scarcely be distinguished in the crowd? (*Institutes*, III, 5, 3-4).

Calvin here is again guilty of presenting a caricature of the Catholic position, whereby it is construed as somehow opposing saints to God or regarding the saints as somehow contributing to the redemption apart from God (the characteristic Protestant dichotomous, or either/or, mindset).

Calvin mistakenly *thinks* this is what Catholics hold. In his commentary on this verse, he repeats the falsehoods about the Catholic position, and even urges readers to hate those who are supposedly deliberately corrupting Holy Writ:

Nor are they ashamed to wrest this passage, with the view of supporting so execrable a blasphemy, as if Paul here affirmed that his sufferings are of avail for expiating the sins of men. . . . I should also be afraid of being suspected of calumny in repeating things so monstrous. . . . Let, therefore, pious readers learn to hate and detest those profane sophists, who thus deliberately corrupt and adulterate the Scriptures."

Albert Barnes exhibits the same misunderstanding of the Catholic interpretation of Colossians 1:24 and similar passages (he was obviously unfamiliar with the decrees of the Council of Trent, or else he read them and did not *understand* them) and refers to the Catholic position as follows:

Their merits might be added to *his* in order to secure the salvation of men, as the Romanists seem to suppose.

Catholics believe that such sufferings truly aid others, just as prayer does (Paul refers to "my sufferings for *your* sake"). No Protestant denies that prayer helps others. Why should not suffering and good works and self-sacrifices undertaken on behalf of others do the same? For prayer is just as much a work as any of these other things. It involves the effort of concentration, mental energy, sometimes moving the lips or raising the hands, and so forth. It is man *doing* something. We are not robots that do whatever God wants us to do at any given moment. We freely cooperate with God, by his grace.

Protestants, therefore, often profoundly misunderstand the Catholic position with regard to these passages and penance in general, and do not sufficiently incorporate all the biblical data to attain a truly biblical doctrine of penance and suffering. Catholic theology, on the other hand, allows for the biblical notion of what St. Alphonsus de Liguori calls "subjective redemption." He provided an eloquent summary of the Catholic conception of penance and vicarious atonement in his *Thoughts on the Passion* (10):

> Can it be that Christ's Passion alone was insufficient to save us? It left nothing more to be done; it was entirely sufficient to save all men. However, for the merits of the Passion to be applied to us, according to St. Thomas (*Summa Theologica*, III, Q. 49, art. 3), we need to cooperate (subjective redemption) by patiently bearing the trials God sends us, so as to become like our head, Christ (in Casciaro, 171).

Chapter Ten

The Communion of Saints

THE IMITATION OF PAUL
AND THE VENERATION OF SAINTS

1 Corinthians 4:16: "I urge you, then, be imitators of me."

Philippians 3:17: "Brethren, join in imitating me, and mark those who so live as you have an example in us."

2 Thessalonians 3:7-9: "For you yourselves know how you ought to imitate us; we were not idle when we were with you, we did not eat anyone's bread without paying, but with toil and labor we worked night and day, that we might not burden any of you. It was not because we have not that right, but to give you in our conduct an example to imitate."

These verses provide a primary biblical basis for the Catholic practice of venerating the saints. We honor the saints because the Bible instructs us to do so (see also Heb. 11). There is nothing wrong or unbiblical in venerating or trying to emulate the saints, unless we were to put them in the place of God, which is idolatry.

When Catholics honor, and keep themselves mindful of, the saints by the use of images and statues, many Protestants immediately conclude that this must be idolatry. They argue that prayerful honor can be given only to God. But the verses just cited show us that proper honor given to saints is not idolatrous and, to the contrary, is even commanded by St. Paul. When we honor and venerate saints, we are giving all the glory to God, who is the source of all saintly qualities.

Martin Luther echoed the Catholic position when he wrote:

> [A]ccording to the law of Moses no other images are forbidden than an image of God which one worships. A crucifix, on the other hand, or any other holy image is not forbidden. . . .
>
> [W]e do not request more than that one permit us to regard a crucifix or a saint's image as a witness, for remembrance, as a sign as that image of Caesar was. Should it not be possible for us without sin to have a crucifix or an image of Mary, as it was for the Jews and Christ himself to have an image of Caesar . . . ? (*Against the Heavenly Prophets in the Matter of Images and Sacraments*, December 1524, LW, 40: 85-86, 96).

Even John Calvin, commenting on Hebrews 12:1 (next page) wrote:

> [E]veryone should be prepared to imitate them; . . . the virtues of the saints are so many testimonies to confirm us, that we, relying on them as our guides and associates, ought to go onward to God with more alacrity.

A. W. Tozer, the much-beloved Christian writer and pastor of the Christian and Missionary Alliance denomination, although denying the invocation of saints, writes luminously of the Mystical Unity of the Body of Christ:

Our Christian brethren who have gone from our sight retain still their place in the universal fellowship. The Church is one. . . . Who is able to complete the roster of the saints? To them we owe a debt of gratitude too great to comprehend. . . . They belong to us, all of them, and we belong to them. They and we . . . are included in the universal fellowship of Christ, and together compose "a royal priesthood, a holy nation, a peculiar people," who enjoy a common but blessed communion of saints (Tozer, 168-170).

Protestants today usually argue that great Christian figures of the past can provide inspiration and example for us in our Christian walk today (per the passages just cited), but they will deny that we ought to venerate them. They say this because they have drawn a false dichotomy between the worship and adoration of God himself and the veneration of those children of God who show forth his glory by displaying the grace that he gave them to be what they are. But it is by no means certain from Scripture that this approach is necessary.

SAINTS IN HEAVEN AS A "CLOUD OF WITNESSES" WATCHING THOSE ON EARTH

Hebrews 12:1: "Therefore, since we are surrounded by so great a cloud of witnesses, let us also lay aside every weight, and sin which clings so closely, and let us run with perseverance the race that is set before us."

Catholics believe that the saints in heaven are aware of happenings on the earth. They are not isolated and removed from earthly realities, but intimately involved in them, as Hebrews 12:1 strongly suggests. *Witnesses* is the Greek word *martus*, from which is derived the English word *martyr*. The reputable Protestant

Greek scholars Marvin Vincent and A. T. Robertson comment on this verse as follows:

> [T]he idea of spectators is implied, and is really the principal idea. The writer's picture is that of an arena in which the Christians whom he addresses are contending in a race, while the vast host of the heroes of faith . . . watches the contest from the encircling tiers of the arena, compassing and overhanging it like a cloud, filled with lively interest and sympathy, and lending heavenly aid (Vincent, IV, 536).
>
> "Cloud of witnesses" *(nephos marturon)* . . . The metaphor refers to the great amphitheater with the arena for the runners and the tiers upon tiers of seats rising up like a cloud. The *martures* here are not mere spectators *(theatai)*, but testifiers (witnesses) who testify from their own experience (11:2, 4-5, 33, 39) to God's fulfilling promises as shown in chapter 11 (Robertson, V, 432).

Protestants try to explain this away, because they seem to fear the notion that saints in heaven and earth have an organic connection. They want simply to "go straight to God" and bypass all the mediating functions of the saints. This makes no more sense than it would to ignore the aid of fellow Christians on earth, whom we ask to lend a hand or pray for us. Albert Barnes provides one example of the Protestant outlook in this regard, in commenting on this passage in his *Notes:*

> It cannot be fairly inferred from this that he means to say that all those ancient worthies were *actually* looking at the conduct of Christians, and saw their conflicts. It is a figurative representation, such as is common, and means that we ought to act as if they were in sight, and cheered us on. How far the spirits of the just who are departed from this world

are permitted to behold what is done on earth — if at all —
is not revealed in the Scriptures.

But Hebrews 12:1 *does* reveal it! Barnes's theology will not let
him see what is right in front of him, even though Robertson and
Vincent see it. How does Barnes know this is "a figurative repre-
sentation"? He provides us no reasons. What inherent limitation
would stop saints in heaven from watching activities on the earth?
Is it not more reasonable to assume (even apart from the scriptural
evidence) that those in heaven will have *at least* as much knowledge of, and interest in, earthly affairs as those on the earth?

Barnes claims that Scripture does not inform us how much
those in heaven know about the earth. Yet Revelation 5:8 and 6:9-
10 show the saints assisting in offering God the "prayers of the
saints" (in which case, presumably, they were *aware* of them) and
praying for a certain outcome of events on the earth.

Protestant Bible scholars Jamieson, Fausset, and Brown, commenting on Revelation 6:10, write:

> The elect (not only on earth, but under Christ's covering,
> and in his presence in Paradise) cry day and night to God,
> who will assuredly, in His own time, avenge his and their
> cause.

Catholic theologian Ludwig Ott wrote:

> The angels and the saints lay the prayers of the holy on
> earth at the feet of God, that is, they support them with
> their intercession as also might be expected from the per-
> manency of charity (1 Cor. 13:8). The propriety of invok-
> ing them logically follows from the fact of their intercession
> (Ott, 318).

The saints are alive, and they love us! Protestants tend to think
that such intercessions or involvements of the dead saints lead

inexorably to idolatry. But they do not, because we are not trying to replace God with saints. Idolatry is worshiping something or someone in place of God Almighty. Venerating a saint or asking him to pray is a fundamentally different concept.

THE INTERCESSION OF THE SAINTS AND
THEIR CONNECTION WITH THE EARTH

Revelation 5:8: "And when he had taken the scroll, the four living creatures and the twenty-four elders fell down before the Lamb, each holding a harp, and with golden bowls full of incense, which are the prayers of the saints."

Revelation 6:9-10: "When he opened the fifth seal, I saw under the altar the souls of those who had been slain for the word of God and for the witness they had borne; they cried out with a loud voice, 'O Sovereign Lord, holy and true, how long before thou wilt judge and avenge our blood on those who dwell upon the earth?' "

Revelation 8:3-4: "And another angel came and stood at the altar with a golden censer; and he was given much incense to mingle with the prayers of all the saints upon the golden altar before the throne; and the smoke of the incense rose with the prayers of the saints from the hand of the angel before God."

Matthew 17:1-3: "And after six days Jesus took with him Peter and James and John his brother, and led them up a high mountain apart. And he was transfigured before them, and his face shone like the sun, and his garments became white as light. And behold, there appeared to them Moses and Elijah, talking with him."

Matthew 27:52-53: "The tombs also were opened, and many bodies of the saints who had fallen asleep were raised, and coming out of the tombs after his resurrection they went into the holy city and appeared to many."

Catholics believe that saints and angels in heaven can pray for us on earth and can hear our intercessory requests, just as people on earth can do; in fact, because the saints are so near to God's presence in heaven, their prayers are more powerful than ours on earth. But most Evangelical Protestants today would deny the saints' intercessory power — and thus claim that any attempt to petition them would be vain at best and idolatrous at worst — as placing superfluous additional mediators between God and mankind.

There is, again, some agreement with the Catholic position among the founders of Protestantism. Martin Luther, in his *Smalcald Articles* of 1537, acknowledged that saints in heaven "perhaps" pray for those on earth, although he denies that they can be invoked or asked to offer prayer:

Although angels in heaven pray for us (as Christ himself also does), and although saints on earth, and perhaps also in heaven, do likewise, it does not follow that we should invoke angels and saints (Part II, Article II, in Tappert, 297).

John Calvin takes a similar view:

They again object, Are those, then, to be deprived of every pious wish, who, during the whole course of their lives, breathed nothing but piety and mercy? . . . [T]here cannot be a doubt that their charity is confined to the communion of Christ's body, and extends no farther than is compatible with the nature of that communion. But though *I grant that in this way they pray for us*, they do not, however, lose their quiescence so as to be distracted with earthly cares: far less are they, therefore, to be invoked by us (*Institutes*, III, 20, 24; emphasis added).

But Calvin continues in the same section, speaking much more like present-day Protestants:

But all such reasons are inapplicable to the dead, with whom the Lord, in withdrawing them from our society, has left us no means of intercourse (Eccles. 9:5, 6), and to whom, so far as we can conjecture, he has left no means of intercourse with us.

Biblical evidence to the contrary was discussed in the preceding section. As for the dead being "withdrawn" from earthly concerns, I would ask Calvin if he were here today: "Why, then, are there so many instances of the dead in Christ having contact with the living, with the full consent of God?" Some examples of this are Moses and Elijah's appearing with Jesus at the Transfiguration (Matt. 17:1-3); the "two witnesses" of Revelation 11:3, whom many commentators believe to be Moses and Elijah also; Samuel's appearance to Saul, prophesying his impending death (1 Sam. 28:12, 14-15; commentators are almost unanimous in asserting that this was actually Samuel); and the many saints who rose from the dead and appeared to many in Jerusalem after Jesus' death (Matt. 27:52-53).

Calvin contradicts himself, however, shortly after he grants that saints in heaven pray for us:

[T]he dead, of whom *we nowhere read that they were commanded to pray for us. The Scripture often exhorts us to offer up mutual prayers; but says not one syllable concerning the dead. . . .* While the Scripture abounds in various forms of prayer, we find no example of this intercession (*Institutes,* III, 20, 27; emphasis added).

Elsewhere, he says flatly:

Of purgatory, the intercession of saints . . . not one syllable can be found in Scripture (*Institutes,* IV, 9, 14).

It is seldom wise to make such sweeping negative statements, because just one counterexample can make them look rather foolish. The counterproof to Calvin's statement lies in the three passages from Revelation cited in this section. Calvin attempts another sort of disproof by claiming that to say the saints intercede for us is to confuse men and angels on the order of being:

We frequently read (they say) of the prayers of angels, and not only so, but the prayers of believers are said to be carried into the presence of God by their hands. . . . How preposterously they confound departed saints with angels is sufficiently apparent from the many different offices by which Scripture distinguishes the one from the other (*Institutes,* III, 20, 23).

This is frivolous logic. All that has to be shown as a commonality is the capacity to *intercede.* Dead saints do not have to have all the characteristics of angels to do that. Calvin's reasoning is as absurd as the following analogy:

1. Someone with a great intellect like Einstein's knows that $2+2=4$.

2. A child of six also knows that $2+2=4$.

3. But in order for a child to know that, he must have all of Einstein's knowledge.

4. Therefore, the child cannot know that $2+2=4$ because he does not have all of Einstein's knowledge.

The false premise obviously lies in proposition number three. Likewise, Calvin's false premise is his implied assumption that saints would need to be like angels in all respects in order to intercede. Apart from the faulty reasoning, Scripture clearly contradicts the assertion, anyway, for Revelation 8:3-4 describes an angel presenting the prayers of the saints to God, and Revelation 5:8 attributes to human beings the same function.

How does Calvin interpret these passages? It is difficult to determine, because he did not comment on them in the *Institutes* (except for one veiled, ambiguous reference above) and did not write a commentary on Revelation. So we will have to examine how other Protestants deal with these fascinating biblical data. Methodists Adam Clarke and John Wesley in their *Commentaries* simply make the prayers presented in 5:8 figurative. Clarke makes a rather curious assertion concerning Revelation 8:3-4:

> It is not said that the angel presents these prayers. He presents the incense, and the prayers ascend *with* it.

But the incense *is* the prayers of the saints in Revelation 5:8, making Clarke's contention implausible. Jamieson, Fausset, and Brown do some eisegesis of their own in commenting on 8:3-4 (capitalization in original):

> How precisely their ministry, in perfuming the prayers of the saints and offering them on the altar of incense, is exercised, we know not, but we do know they are not to be prayed TO. . . . It is not the saints who give the angel the incense; nor are their prayers identified with the incense; nor do they offer their prayers to him. Christ alone is the Mediator through whom, and to whom, prayer is to be offered.

How, indeed, do we *know* that the angels are not asked to intercede? For it stands to reason that they would be offering the prayers of the saints only if they were asked to — otherwise those prayers would not be, in a sense, theirs to offer.

Lastly, the fact that Christ is mediator is not questioned by anyone. Asking a saint in heaven to pray for us no more interferes with the unique mediation of Christ than does asking a person on earth to pray for us. We always pray in Christ, through his power, and to him, whether it is directly to him, or by means of another person or angel, in heaven or on earth.

The (false) dichotomy between Christ's mediation and human or angelic mediation need not be drawn at all; it arises only because of the Protestant's needless alarmism at God's making use of creatures to fulfill his purposes. Jamieson, Fausset, and Brown's comment on Revelation 5:8 exhibits even more of a sort of "fortress mentality":

> This gives not the least sanction to Rome's dogma of our praying to saints. Though *they* be employed by God in some way unknown to us to present our prayers (nothing is said of their *interceding* for us), yet *we* are told to pray only to Him (Rev. 19:10; 22:8, 9).

We are not told in Scripture that we cannot ask someone in heaven to pray for us. Saints in heaven are more alive and aware and far holier than we are. They watch us (Heb. 12:1). They are aware of earthly happenings (Rev. 6:9-10). They can certainly be given extraordinary capacities for knowledge by God; there is nothing implausible or intrinsically impossible or unbiblical in that notion at all.

St. Paul states about the afterlife in heaven:

> **1 Corinthians 13:12:** "For now we see in a mirror dimly, but then face-to-face. Now I know in part; then I shall understand fully, even as I have been fully understood."

Therefore, they can pray for us, and we can ask for their prayers. We know that they can come back to earth (from the four examples given earlier). Are we to believe that when such saints come to earth, they can pray, but immediately upon returning to heaven they cannot once again? And if they can present our prayers, why is it so inconceivable that they could intercede for us?

Albert Barnes in his comment on both Revelation 5:8 and 8:3 draws some hairsplitting distinctions that would make the most skillful lawyer envious:

> The representation there [Revelation 8:3] undoubtedly is that the angel is *employed* in presenting the prayers of the saints which were offered on earth before the throne. It is most natural to interpret the passage before us [Revelation 5:8] in the same way. . . . It is not said that *they* offer the prayers themselves, but that they offer *incense* as representing the prayers of the saints.

Much more sensible and plausible is part of his comment on Revelation 6:9-10:

> *The souls of them that were slain.* That had been put to death by persecution. This is one of the incidental proofs in the Bible that the soul does not cease to exist at death, and also that it does not cease to be conscious, or does not sleep till the resurrection. These souls of the martyrs are represented as still in existence; as remembering what had occurred on the earth; as interested in what was now taking place; as engaged in prayer; and as manifesting earnest desires for the Divine interposition to avenge the wrongs which they had suffered.

But then, Barnes's Protestant bias comes over him again:

> [N]or are we to suppose that the injured and the wronged in heaven actually pray for vengeance on those who wronged

them, or that the redeemed in heaven will continue to pray with reference to things on the earth; but it may be fairly inferred from this that there will be *as real* a remembrance of the wrongs of the persecuted, the injured, and the oppressed, *as if* such prayer were offered there.

Peter Berger, an eminent Lutheran sociologist, discusses with great insight the difference between Protestantism and Catholicism with regard to the Communion of Saints:

If compared with the "fullness" of the Catholic universe, Protestantism appears as a radical truncation, a reduction to "essentials" at the expense of a vast wealth of religious contents. . . . Protestantism may be described in terms of an immense shrinkage in the scope of the sacred in reality, as compared with its Catholic adversary. . . . The immense network of intercession that unites the Catholic in this world with the saints and, indeed, with all departed souls disappears as well. Protestantism ceased praying for the dead.

The Catholic lives in a world in which the sacred is mediated to him through a variety of channels — the sacraments of the church, the intercession of the saints, the recurring eruption of the "supernatural" in miracles — a vast continuity of being between the seen and the unseen. Protestantism abolished most of these mediations. It broke the continuity, cut the umbilical cord between heaven and earth (Berger, 111-112).

Protestants are very reluctant to speak about these departed saints at all, for fear that it would raise them to a "godlike" status or detract from God's sole glory and majesty; or perhaps that it would lead them dangerously close to necromancy. As we have seen, this reluctance runs counter to much biblical indication otherwise. In this, as in so many instances, I believe that the underlying negative or skeptical attitude is rooted in a fear or suspicion that to act in "Catholic" ways would be to yield ground to Catholics and to start down a slippery slope leading inexorably to Rome. It is a defensive "fortress mentality." But I would contend that all Christians must yield to the biblical examples and commands, whether the issue at hand outwardly appears "Protestant" or "Catholic."

Catholics who venture out into the ground of apologetics and sharing their faith with Protestants will encounter this attitude over and over, and need to be aware of how to counter it with solid biblical argumentation and simple logic. As Peter Berger noted above, Protestantism is characterized by "an immense shrinkage in the scope of the sacred in reality."

The mysterious, the miraculous, the sacramental, and other similar elements are minimized in many sectors of Protestantism. The overwhelming emphasis is on the individual in relationship to God, and the "Word" (construed as the Bible alone). That is simply not in accord with the Bible and historical Christianity. Therefore, Catholics who try to defend these beliefs need to show that they are rooted in the Bible, not merely petrified and arbitrary "[Catholic] traditions of men."

Chapter Eleven

Relics and Sacramentals

ELISHA'S BONES RAISE A MAN FROM THE DEAD

2 Kings 13:20-21: "So Elisha died, and they buried him. Now bands of Moabites used to invade the land in the spring of the year. And as a man was being buried, lo, a marauding band was seen and the man was cast into the grave of Elisha; and as soon as the man touched the bones of Elisha, he revived, and stood on his feet."

Catholics believe that physical matter can be a conveyor of spiritual grace. This is the foundation for the use of relics (objects associated with saints) and sacramentals (sacred or devotional objects). Catholic apologist Bertrand Conway elaborates:

The Catholic Church does not teach that there is any magical virtue or any curative efficacy in the relic itself. The Church merely says, following the Scriptures, that they are often the occasion of God's miracles. In the Old Law we read of the veneration of the Jews for the bones of Joseph (Exod. 13:19; Josh. 24:32), and of the prophet Eliseus [Elisha] which raised a dead man to life (2 Kings 13:21) (Conway, 373).

As John Henry Newman so eloquently put it in his profoundly influential work *Essay on the Development of Christian Doctrine*, this belief follows logically from the doctrine of the Incarnation:

> Christianity . . . taught that the Highest had in [the] flesh died on the Cross, and that His blood had an expiatory power; moreover, that He had risen again in that flesh, and had carried that flesh with Him into heaven, and that from that flesh, glorified and deified in Him, He never would be divided. As a first consequence of these awful doctrines comes that of the resurrection of the bodies of His saints, and of their future glorification with Him; next, that of the sanctity of their relics (*Development*, Pt. II, ch. X, sect. 1, 401-402).

Protestants often act as if matter and spirit are naturally opposed to each other (with matter being evil or less good than spirit). Catholics, of course, strongly disagree with this outlook. Thomas Howard, writing also as an Anglican on the verge of conversion to Catholicism, picked up the theme of the unbiblical Protestant tendency to set matter against spirit:

> By avoiding the dangers of magic and idolatry on the one hand, Evangelicalism runs itself very near the shoals of Manichaeanism on the other — the view, that is, that pits the spiritual against the physical (Howard, 35).

This tendency in some strains of modern Evangelicalism is seen, for example, in silly legalisms about dancing being immoral, or puritanistic notions of sex (even married sex) being a "dirty" or evil thing. It is seen in the reluctance to accept the Eucharist as substantially the Body and Blood of Christ (along with, of course, opposition to relics and things like holy water and crucifixes).

Keeping mindful of this background, let us look at some examples of how Protestants have interpreted 2 Kings 13:20-21. Adam

Clarke, in his commentary, admits, somewhat typically, it seems, the validity of the principle (that God can work spiritually through matter), but then immediately proceeds irrationally to mock the Catholic belief-system concerning relics that *derives* from it:

> This shows that the prophet did not perform his miracles by any powers of his own, but by the power of God; and he chose to honor his servant, by making even his bones the instrument of another miracle after his death. This is the first, and I believe the last, account of a true miracle performed by the bones of a dead man; and yet on it and such like the whole system of miraculous working relics has been founded by the popish Church.

With this sort of mentality, explicit biblical precedents and proof texts for any Christian belief or practice can be deemed irrelevant. Clarke's underlying assumption seems to be that the only criterion we have for determining whether a belief is true or false (regardless of the biblical data) is whether the "popish Church" espouses it. If it does, it must be false.

Presbyterian Matthew Henry, in his very well-known commentary, manages to recognize the implications of the verse without adding a gratuitous swipe against the "papists":

> This great miracle . . . was also a plain indication of another life after this. When Elisha died, there was not an end of him, for then he could not have done this. From operation we may infer existence. . . . Elijah was honored *in* his departure. Elisha was honored *after* his departure.

It must be noted again that veneration of the saints and their relics is essentially different from the kind worship or adoration reserved for God alone, in that it is a high honor given to something or someone *because* of the grace revealed or demonstrated in them from God. The relic (and the saint from whom it is derived) reflects the greatness of God just as a masterpiece of art or music reflects the greatness of the artist or composer.

Therefore, in such veneration, it is *God* being honored. The saint is venerated only insofar as he reflects God's grace and holiness. To worship as divine a saint or relic is not following Catholic teaching, which fully agrees with Protestantism with regard to the evil of idolatry.

In the passage from 2 Kings, matter clearly imparts God's miraculous grace. That is all that is needed for Catholics reasonably and scripturally to hold such relics in the highest regard and honor (veneration). It is not necessary for the entire doctrine of veneration to be spelled out in the verse, only the fundamental assumption behind it (matter can convey grace), which is the basis for the Catholic belief and practice.

Many Protestants (including Martin Luther himself, Lutherans, Methodists, Anglicans, Churches of Christ) accept this principle with regard to the waters of baptism, which, so they hold, cause spiritual regeneration to occur, even in an infant.

As for the graven-image prohibition of Exodus 20:4, what God was forbidding there was *idolatry*: making a stone or block of wood into a god. The Jews were forbidden to have idols (which all their neighbors had), and God told them not to make an image of him because he revealed himself as a spirit. The KJV and RSV Bible versions use the term *graven image* at Exodus 20:4, but many of the more recent translations render the word as *idol* (e.g., NASB, NRSV, NIV, CEV).

Context makes it very clear that idolatry is being condemned. The next verse states: "You shall not bow down to them or worship them" (NIV, NRSV). In other words, mere blocks of stone or wood ("them") are not to be worshiped, as that is gross idolatry, and the inanimate objects are not God. This does not absolutely preclude, however, the notion of an *icon*, where God is worshiped with the help of a visual aid.

Idolatry is a matter of disobedience in the heart toward the one true God. We do not always need an image to have an idol. Most idols today are nonvisual: money, sex, lust for power, convenience, our own pride or intellects; there are all sorts of idols. Anything that displaces God as the most important thing in our life and the universe is an idol.

Catholics and Orthodox worship Jesus through images (including crosses, crucifixes, and statues of Jesus), and we venerate saints through images. The common Protestant objection and opposition to veneration of images or of relics (as in this case) is as silly as saying that a person raising his hands toward God in worship and praise at church is worshiping the ceiling. That person may not have an image of God in his mind, but he uses the symbolism of "upward" as being directed toward God (yet God is everywhere, so one could just as correctly stretch his arms downward or sideways).

We are physical creatures; God became man, and so by the principle of the Incarnation and sacramentalism, the physical becomes involved in the spiritual. Icons and relics are both based on these presuppositions.

MORE BIBLICAL RELICS: ELIJAH'S MANTLE, PETER'S SHADOW, AND PAUL'S HANDKERCHIEF

2 Kings 2:11-14: "And as they still went on and talked, behold, a chariot of fire and horses of fire separated the two of them. And Elijah went up by a whirlwind into heaven. And Elisha saw it and he cried, 'My father, my father! The chariots of Israel and its horsemen!' And he saw him no more. Then he took hold of his own clothes and rent them in two pieces. And he took up the mantle of Elijah that had fallen from him, and went back and stood on the bank of the Jordan. Then he took the mantle of

Elijah that had fallen from him, and struck the water, saying, 'Where is the Lord, the God of Elijah?' And when he had struck the water, the water was parted to the one side and to the other; and Elisha went over."

Acts 5:15-16: "[T]hey even carried out the sick into the streets, and laid them on beds and pallets, that as Peter came by at least his shadow might fall on some of them. The people also gathered from the towns around Jerusalem, bringing the sick and those afflicted with unclean spirits, and they were all healed."

Acts 19:11-12: "And God did extraordinary miracles by the hands of Paul, so that handkerchiefs or aprons were carried away from his body to the sick, and diseases left them and the evil spirits came out of them" (cf. Matt. 9:20-22).

Elisha's bones were what Catholics call a "first-class relic": part of the person himself. These passages, on the other hand, offer examples of second-class relics: items that have power because they were *connected* with a holy person (Elijah's mantle and even St. Peter's shadow), and third-class relics: something that has merely *touched* a holy person or first-class relic of a person (handkerchiefs that had touched St. Paul).

Surveying a few examples of Protestant commentary on these verses, we find no real substantive objections. Matthew Henry refers to Elisha's taking up Elijah's mantle "not as a sacred relic to be worshiped." Yet Catholics do not worship relics, but venerate them, because they represent a saint who, in turn, reflects the grace and holiness of God. Henry offers no essential disproof that this is indeed a relic, only a potshot against a straw man.

God ultimately performs all miracles by his power, but in this case and many others he uses physical objects to do so (e.g., Moses' staff, a Temple made of stone and wood). Belief that God can use something in his creation for a miraculous purpose does not in any way imply that God is not the cause of the miracle. Adam Clarke, failing to grasp this, cynically comments on St. Peter's shadow, offering seven "disproofs" of relics:

> A popish writer, assuming that the shadow of Peter actually cured all on which it was projected, argues from this precarious principle in favor of the wonderful efficacy of relics! . . . Now, before this conclusion can be valid, it must be proved: 1. that the shadow of Peter did actually cure the sick; 2. that this was a virtue common to all the apostles; 3. that all eminent saints possess the same virtue; 4. that the bones, etc., of the dead possess the same virtue with the shadow of the living; 5. that those whom they term saints were actually such; 6. that miracles of healing have been wrought by their relics; 7. that touching these relics necessarily produces the miraculous healing as they suppose the shadow of Peter to have done. . . . [N]o evidence can be drawn from this that any virtue is resident in the relics of reputed or real saints, by which miraculous influence may be conveyed.

Clarke's analysis is consistent with modern Evangelical thinking on most points. Not many Evangelicals today would deny the recorded miracle of Peter's shadow curing someone, nor deny that apostles had extraordinary healing powers. But they would be in perfect accord with him in their general antipathy to the concept of relics. They take a very dim view of preserving the bones of saints, yet they have not offered a way, that I have seen, to reconcile the passage about Elisha's bones. I shall briefly reply to Clarke's seven points:

1. That St. Peter's shadow was instrumental in healings is at least as reasonable and plausible an assumption from the text as denying it was.

2 and 3. Whether all the Apostles and saints possessed this characteristic is logically irrelevant to the fact that it occurred here with Peter and thus sets a biblical precedent for Catholic belief in second-class relics.

4. This is a *non sequitur*. The evidence for bones also potentially having such power can be seen from the example of Elisha.

5. Whether a person was a saint is a matter of rigorous historical investigation by the Catholic Church (usually taking many years).

6. Whether miracles have occurred historically as a result of relics is also a matter of historical substantiation. They certainly *have*, but proof of that is beyond our purview here.

7. Catholics do not say that healing *necessarily* follows from contact with a relic, but only that it *may*, and that this is one legitimate means that God may in some instances use to heal and otherwise bestow grace upon sinful men.

Clarke's case against relics based on this scriptural passage is a combination of irrelevancies, straw men, wrongheaded analogies, conclusions that do not follow, unwarranted demands, and outright skepticism of the occurrence of the supernatural (many Protestants, called *cessationists*, believe that *all* miracles ceased with the Apostles). Matthew Henry, in his commentary on Peter's shadow, is not nearly so skeptical as Clarke:

> [I]f such miracles were wrought by Peter's shadow, we have reason to think they were so by the other apostles, as by the handkerchiefs from Paul's body (ch. xix. 12), no doubt both being with an actual intention in the minds of the apostles thus to heal; so that it is absurd to infer hence a healing virtue in the relics of saints that are dead and gone.

This is excellent and no different from the Catholic view, except for the last clause, which does not at all logically or biblically follow. Rather than recognize this instance as a clear proof of the principle of relics, Henry belittles relics as absurd with one portion of a sentence — itself containing an altogether unproven assumption: that in order for a healing to occur, it must be the *intention* of a person performing it (thus ruling out miracles as a result of relics, by definition).

But whence comes this criterion? For to the contrary, Elisha was dead, yet his bones still raised a man from the dead. Elisha certainly could have had no intention of healing that person (unless he did so from heaven). Henry himself grasps the absurd implications when commenting on Elisha's bones, but contradicts himself here and cannot bring himself to admit anything that might have a "Catholic odor" to it.

Catholics, however (like the overwhelming number of those in the early Church), are not limited by this bias against matter as a purveyor of grace and the notion of relics itself, and so can accept the Bible's teaching, wherever it leads. And that teaching is that relics can and have been used by God to heal people and otherwise communicate his grace to them.

Chapter Twelve

Purgatory and Prayers for the Dead

A BIBLICAL ARGUMENT FOR PURGATORY

1 Corinthians 3:11-15: "For no other foundation can anyone lay than that which is laid, which is Jesus Christ. Now, if anyone builds on the foundation with gold, silver, precious stones, wood, hay, straw — each man's work will become manifest; for the Day will disclose it, because it will be revealed with fire, and the fire will test what sort of work each one has done. If the work which any man has built on the foundation survives, he will receive a reward. If any man's work is burned up, he will suffer loss, though he himself will be saved, but only as through fire."

It will be an extremely serious business when we meet God face-to-face. There will not be any more "imputation" — merely "covering over" of sins — then. No, to stand in his presence we must be literally, actually sinless, because that is how we were created to be in the first place, in his image. We have to be cleansed of *actual* sin ("sanctification," in Protestant theological language).

There is no Protestant-Catholic difference on this particular point, from either side. The only difference is a *quantitative* one:

Catholics think this cleansing will involve a *process*, like our life on earth. And that process of sanctification can continue after death: in purgatory. Protestants, on the other hand, seem to think this all occurs in an instant.

One Protestant I was interacting with stated, "God will certainly remove the filth of the flesh prior to the resurrection of our bodies." Precisely, and that is what purgatory is; no Protestant should have the slightest objection to it. The big beef is (or should be) about how long this removal of filth takes, and exactly when it occurs. Both sides agree that the thing itself does occur in some fashion.

Obviously, human beings want to avoid suffering as much as possible. The Protestant view, whether consciously or not, often in practice appeals to the natural human desire to avoid suffering: instant heaven, instant glorification at death, instant salvation, instant eternal security and assurance of our saved status, and so forth. The problem with this desire is that the Bible constantly refers to suffering as a means of attaining to holiness and wisdom (e.g., Rom. 5:3-5; 2 Cor. 1:5, 12:7-9; James 1:2-4, 12, 5:10-11; 1 Pet. 5:10).

Childbirth offers a close parallel to purgatory, I believe. I have seen the births of my four children, and at each one, I marveled at how my wife went through such tremendous agony, yet had a peace and joy even during the suffering, and an ecstatic joy upon the birth and seeing her child, immediately forgetting what had just gone on. I believe that is how *we* will feel after emerging from purgatory finally clean and gazing upon our Lord's beautiful and glorious face.

There will not be a moment's thought then as to whether the preparatory suffering was worth it (Rom. 8:18). And we will understand even more fully than while in purgatory why it was necessary and wonder how we could ever have been so silly to have ever denied the necessity of it for a moment. The great Anglican apologist (and my favorite writer), C. S. Lewis, wrote:

I believe in purgatory. . . . Our souls *demand* purgatory, don't they? Would it not break the heart if God said to us, "It is true, my son, that your breath smells and your rags drip with mud and slime, but we are charitable here and no one will upbraid you with these things, nor draw away from you. Enter into the joy"? Should we not reply, "With submission, sir, and if there is no objection, I'd *rather* be cleaned first." "It may hurt, you know" — "Even so, sir" (Lewis, 108-109).

John Calvin vainly attempts to make 1 Corinthians 3:11-15 not refer to the Day of Judgment (so as to escape any implication of purgatory):

[T]he Spirit is that fire by which they will be proved. This proof Paul calls the *day of the Lord;* using a term common in Scripture. For the day of the Lord is said to take place whenever he in some way manifests his presence to men, his face being specially said to shine when his truth is manifested. It has now been proved that Paul has no idea of any other fire than the trial of the Holy Spirit (*Institutes*, III, 5, 9).

This is a clever attempt to evade the inherent eschatological, judgmental aspects of this passage, but it fails. Modern biblical scholarship does not agree that *day* here has to do with every manifestation of the Spirit, but rather, to the Day of Judgment. Hence, writes the linguist Gerhard Kittel:

[Gk., *hemera*] In Paul the "day" is the great day of judgment for the church (1 Cor. 1:8) or himself (2 Cor. 1:14) as well as non-Christians; it serves as an ethical incentive. . . . In the absolute, "day" is the day of judgment in 1 Thess. 5:5; 1 Cor. 3:13; Heb. 10:25 (cf. "that day" in Matt. 7:22 etc. and "great day" in Jude 6; Rev. 6:17, etc.). The day of Christ's manifestation and the day of judgment are, of course, the same (Kittel, 310).

The Baptist Greek scholar A. T. Robertson likewise regards the "day" in 1 Corinthians 3:13 (contra Calvin's "proved" view) as "the day of judgment as in 1 Thess. 5:4 . . . Rom. 13:12; Heb. 10:25" (Robertson, IV, 97). Marvin Vincent also believes that St. Paul had in mind "a final and decisive test at the day of judgment, when the true value of each teacher's work shall be manifested" (Vincent, III, 203).

Robertson, however, echoes Calvin's common shortcoming of describing fairly accurately what Catholics believe occurs in purgatory, yet denying, for no observable reason, that the passage could pertain to purgatory:

> There is no escape from this final testing. . . . This metaphor of fire was employed in the O.T. (Dan. 7:9; Mal. 4:1) and by John the Baptist (Matt. 3:12; Luke 3:16). It is a metaphor that must not be understood as purgatorial, but simple testing. . . . The man's work (*ergon*) is burned up. . . . But he himself shall be saved (*autos de sothesetai*). Eternal salvation, but not by purgatory. His work is burned up completely and hopelessly, but he himself escapes destruction because he is really a saved man (Robertson, IV, 97-98).

This is about as descriptive and accurate a summary of purgatory as could be expected from a Baptist, but of course, the doctrine itself is impermissible, so Robertson cannot go there. He does not inform us why (if indeed he has a reason), but in the meantime he describes, almost despite himself, why the text is an excellent proof indeed for purgatory.

Finding corroboration of Catholic views like the above statement is often the joy of Catholics (especially apologists like me), when consulting Protestant biblical scholarship. The scholars themselves are usually not aware of such corroboration, and sometimes even deny it in so many words. This is the sort of ironic result that ignorance of Catholic doctrine, even among highly educated men devoted to the Bible (and no doubt also to God, in most cases), often brings about. On the other end of the spectrum, however, Adam Clarke opines:

> The popish writers . . . might with equal propriety have applied it to the discovery of the longitude, the perpetual motion, or the philosopher's stone; because it speaks just as much of the former as it does of any of the latter. The fire mentioned here is to try the man's work, not to purify his soul; but the dream of purgatory refers to the purging in another state what left this impure; not the work of the man, but the man himself; but here the fire is said to try the work: ergo, purgatory is not meant.

I submit that this is straining at gnats. James White tries the same approach: the text talks about works, not sins (as if the two had no relation to each other, despite the many passages concerning judgment, dealt with earlier); therefore, he concludes, it is not about purgatory (White, 193). Matthew Henry does likewise, preceded by the following most unscholarly observation:

> On this passage of Scripture the papists found their doctrine of purgatory, which is certainly hay and stubble: a doctrine never originally fetched from Scripture, but invented in barbarous ages, to feed the avarice and ambition of the clergy, at the cost of those who would rather part with their money than their lusts, for the salvation of their souls. It can have no countenance from this text.

But we need not indulge Henry's speculations about the nefarious motives that caused "barbarous" medieval Catholics supposedly to invent purgatory. St. Augustine was certainly as good an exegete as any of the men just mentioned and is generally highly regarded by Protestants. Yet he often espouses the doctrine of purgatory (and he lived long before the Middle Ages):

In this life may You cleanse me and make me such that I have no need of the corrective fire, which is for those who are saved, but as if by fire. . . . For it is said: "He shall be saved, but as if by fire" [1 Cor. 3:15] . . . plainly, though we be saved by fire, that fire will be more severe than anything a man can suffer in this life (*Explanations of the Psalms*, 37, 3; in Jurgens, III, 17).

[A]fter this life he will have either purgatorial fire or eternal punishment (*Genesis Defended Against the Manicheans*, 2, 20, 30; in Jurgens, III, 38).

But not all who suffer temporal punishments after death will come to eternal punishments, which are to follow after that judgment (*The City of God*, 21, 13; in Jurgens, III, 105).

[S]ome of the faithful may be saved, some more slowly and some more quickly in the greater or lesser degree in which they loved the good things that perish — through a certain purgatorial fire *[per ignem quemdam purgatorium]* (*The Enchiridion of Faith, Hope, and Love*, 18, 69; in Jurgens, III, 149).

Alas, we are fortunate to have John Calvin to correct the hapless, gullible St. Augustine and the many Church Fathers who believed in purgatory or some reasonable facsimile thereof:

Surely, any man endowed with a modicum of wisdom easily recognizes that whatever he reads among the ancient writers concerning this matter was allowed because of public custom and common ignorance. I admit that the fathers themselves were also carried off into error. For heedless credulity commonly deprives men's minds of judgment (in McNeill, *Institutes*, III, 5, 10).

Elsewhere, Calvin practically mocks St. Augustine, noting that in his famous *Confessions*, the great Church Father had written about his mother, Monica, wanting to be remembered in the Mass after she died (IX, 11). Augustine offered a lengthy, quite moving, obviously deeply felt prayer for her after her death (IX, 13). But here is what Calvin has to say about this event:

> This was obviously an old woman's request, which the son did not test by the norm of Scripture; but he wished to be approved by others for his natural affection (in McNeill, *Institutes*, III, 5, 10).

Calvin seems to think that his own ability to read hearts and minds (and to judge even the greatest and most intellectually brilliant of saints) is equal to his exegetical abilities. I submit that both were not quite as lofty and unquestionable as he imagined. Purgatory is a biblical doctrine.

BAPTISM FOR THE DEAD: THE MOST "UN-PROTESTANT" VERSE IN THE BIBLE

1 Corinthians 15:29: "Otherwise, what do people mean by being baptized on behalf of the dead? If the dead are not raised at all, why are people baptized on their behalf?"

Many Protestant commentators (I will provide some examples shortly) think this is one of the most obscure passages in the New Testament, even the single most mysterious passage. As such, it is particularly relevant for our study. St. Francis de Sales (1567-1622), the great Catholic apologist and Doctor of the Church, exegeted this passage in the following way (which would be quite sufficient to make any Protestant very uneasy):

> This passage properly understood evidently shows that it was the custom of the primitive Church to watch, pray, fast, for the souls of the departed. For, firstly, in the Scriptures to

be baptized is often taken for afflictions and penances; as in St. Luke chapter 12 [12:50] . . . and in St. Mark chapter 10 [10:38-39] . . . in which places our Lord calls pains and afflictions baptism [cf. Matt. 3:11, 20:22-3; Luke 3:16].

This, then, is the sense of that Scripture: if the dead rise not again, what is the use of mortifying and afflicting oneself, of praying and fasting for the dead? And indeed this sentence of St. Paul resembles that of 2 Maccabees 12:44: *It is superfluous and vain to pray for the dead if the dead rise not again* (St. Francis de Sales, 368).

With this Catholic explanation in mind, I will try to provide some insight into the way some Protestants interpret this passage, by recalling a fascinating, enjoyable Internet dialogue I recently had with six Protestant opponents. I will give the highlights, as an example of what Protestants try to do when they are confronted with a biblical text that cannot be harmonized with their theology.

One person argued that here Paul was showing the inconsistency of a literal practice of baptizing people on behalf of others who had died. I replied that the context falsified this interpretation. St. Paul's statement, whatever it means, is used as a rhetorical argument favoring the resurrection of the dead, not as an anomalous, incongruous example within the context of a positive affirmation of resurrection.

The whole of chapter 15 deals with Jesus' Resurrection and the resurrection of his followers. St. Paul's point is that the Christian life of toil and suffering is pointless if there is no resurrection and if Jesus himself did not rise again (15:14, 17, 19), in which case we might as well be hedonists (15:32). After he makes his statement in 15:29, he proclaims in the next verse, "Why am I in peril every hour?"

In other words, "Why do I go through what I go through, if not for the hope of the resurrection and eternal life [cf. 15:32]?"

His example of baptism was one of several practices that make sense only if there is a resurrection. By analogy, then, it is not presented as an inconsistency at all, but as an acceptable practice in light of the resurrection, just like his "peril" and dying "every day" (15:31).

A second person suggested that this passage was talking about those who had been so impressed by Christian martyrs that they decided to become believers and get baptized. Another denied that there was any such practice going on, whatever it was. He thought that the passage meant that believers were identifying in baptism with a dead man — Jesus Christ — and were "dead to the world but were alive to Christ."

This latter interpretation fails utterly, I think, because the passage does not say we were baptized *in* Christ or *with* him, as other baptism passages suggest; rather, it says people are baptized *on behalf of* the dead — an entirely different concept. Obviously, our Lord Jesus needs nothing done on his behalf. Secondly, "the dead" seems to me to be a corporate term, not referring to Jesus alone. It would be exceedingly strange to refer to Jesus as "the dead." Thus, linguist Joseph H. Thayer informs us that the use of the Greek *nekros* in this verse is a plural application, referring to "the dead" as a group (Thayer, 423).

This interpretation is also contradicted throughout chapter 15, because when Paul refers to Jesus, he repeatedly uses the title "Christ" (15:3-4, 12-17, 20), whereas "the dead" clearly refers to the resurrection of us poor, miserable created human beings (in contradistinction to the Resurrection of Jesus Christ, e.g., 15:12-13, 15-16, 52). The distinction between the two could not be clearer, with Paul often contrasting them in the very same verse.

My opponent did not deal with any of these points. He just insisted that I was "begging the question" — engaging in circular reasoning. He continued protesting in this fashion and graciously offering me lessons in elementary logic, but I kept to exegesis and hermeneutics. I contended that my notion fit in perfectly well with the schema of the chapter because Paul was making a rhetorical argument having to do with the fact that there are folks who are resurrected and alive in the afterlife. We could paraphrase his rhetorical question: "Why do something for their sakes if they are not there in the first place?" That made perfect sense to me.

But my friend suggested an awkward reading of the phrase "the dead" and tried to apply it to Jesus' Resurrection, even though Paul everywhere else in the chapter used it as a term for the dead generally speaking, and contrasted it to Christ several times. I suggested that this indicated exegetical desperation on his part.

He appealed to Calvin's commentary to support his argument, but he would not respond to my critiques. (Why have the discussion in the first place, then, I wondered?) I consulted Calvin and found that he did not say that "the dead" refers to Christ, which was a major component of my friend's position.

One of the basic mistakes was that everyone was assuming that St. Paul was referring to *water* baptism, when it is not necessary to do so simply by virtue of the word *baptism,* which has a few meanings in Scripture. Biblically, and in Catholicism, it is nonsensical to be water-baptized for someone else, because (for Catholics, Orthodox, and several species of Protestants such as Lutherans, Anglicans, Church of Christ, and so forth) it confers regeneration, and a dead person is either regenerate or not, beyond the help of the earthly sacraments.

No "proxy baptism" will change that fact after they are dead. Even if one denies baptismal regeneration, "proxy baptism" makes no sense because the power and graces conferred by baptism apply only to the one receiving them.

What does make sense, though, is the "penitential" interpretation (expressed by St. Francis de Sales above), because that easily harmonizes with the parallel passage in Maccabees about prayer for the dead. The problem here is that Protestant theology has no place for such thought, and so it is ruled out from the outset. Thus, the text remains mysterious for Protestants because of, in this instance, the false preconception they bring to it. I opined that it would be better for Protestants simply to admit ignorance about the passage than to special plead in order to avoid at all costs a "Catholic" interpretation.

This was how the discussion went. There was no true constructive interaction. They gave their exegesis; I gave mine. I critiqued theirs, but they would not follow up my criticisms in any significant or in-depth fashion. My Protestant friends scarcely even tried to argue against my interpretation at all; the one person simply declared it worthless and logically circular. He appealed to Calvin, but I showed how his view *contradicted* Calvin at a crucial point. So it often goes in Catholic-Protestant discussion.

Calvin's own take in his *Commentaries* is rather implausible, in my opinion:

> [T]o be *baptized for the dead* will mean — to be baptized so as to profit the dead — not the living. . . . [I]f a catechumen, who had already in his heart embraced the Christian faith, saw that death was impending over him, he asked baptism, partly for his own consolation, and partly with a view to the edification of his brethren. . . . They were, then, *baptized for the dead*, inasmuch as it could not be of any service to them in this world, and the very occasion of their asking baptism was that they despaired of life.

In other words, Calvin would apply the "baptism for the dead to the individual's *own death* (that is, the one who is baptized), as he is about to die, and the baptism therefore applies mostly to the dead." This might make some sense insofar as we do things that affect our life hereafter, but this interpretation is very strained, given the language of the passage. Calvin obviously resorts to this forced explanation because for him, it makes no sense for baptism to apply to anyone other than the one receiving it. St. Francis de Sales's suggestion that other types of baptism are here referred to is much more plausible.

Other well-known Protestant commentators offer no more light. Matthew Henry says that the verse is a "very obscure passage, which, though it consists of no more than three words, besides the articles, has had more than three times three senses put on it by interpreters." Albert Barnes observes, "There is, perhaps, no passage of the New Testament in respect to which there has been a greater variety of interpretation than this; and the views of expositors now by no means harmonize in regard to its meaning."

He outlines five major schools of thought, but none of them includes the Catholic interpretation, as given by St. Francis de Sales. Adam Clarke also considers it a puzzling verse (but arguably it is mostly so because of Protestant theological presuppositions):

> This is certainly the most difficult verse in the New Testament; for, notwithstanding the greatest and wisest men have labored to explain it, there are to this day nearly as many different interpretations of it as there are interpreters . . . a vast number of discordant and conflicting opinions.

After offering about eight internally inconsistent and implausible thoughts on the passage, he gives his own tentative reading (equally as untenable as Calvin's):

> [A]s they receive baptism as an emblem of death in voluntarily going under the water, so they receive it as an emblem of the resurrection unto eternal life, in coming up out of the water; thus they are baptized for the dead, in perfect faith of the resurrection.
>
> This verse offers a classic example of Protestant confusion and incoherence in the face of a biblical passage that appears to be utterly at odds with Protestant theology.

THE CASE OF ONESIPHORUS:
DID ST. PAUL PRAY FOR A DEAD MAN?

2 Timothy 1:16-18: "May the Lord grant mercy to the household of Onesiphorus, for he often refreshed me; he was not ashamed of my chains, but when he arrived in Rome he searched for me eagerly and found me — may the Lord grant him to find mercy from the Lord on that Day — and you well know all the service he rendered at Ephesus."

Catholics believe in prayers for the dead, in order to aid them in their journey through purgatory to heaven. In fact, praying for the dead makes sense only if some sort of purgatory or intermediate state is presupposed, because it would be futile to pray for those in hell (prayer cannot help them; it is too late) and unnecessary to pray for those in heaven (they have everything they need). This verse offers one probable biblical support for this belief.

The Anglican C. S. Lewis believed in prayers for the dead:

Of course I pray for the dead. The action so spontaneous, so all but inevitable, that only the most compulsive theological case against it would deter me. . . . At our age the majority of those we love best are dead. What sort of intercourse with God could I have if what I love best were unmentionable to Him?

[E]ven in Heaven some perpetual increase of beatitude, reached by a continually more ecstatic self-surrender, without the possibility of failure but not perhaps without its own ardors and exertions . . . might be supposed (Lewis, 107-108).

Thomas Howard (also writing as an Anglican) concurs:

The notion that a man's whole story is finished at the precise point of physical death and his destiny fixed and sealed is not made clear in the Bible. The text, ". . . it is appointed unto man once to die, but after this the judgment," in Hebrews 9:27, which is often advanced in discussions on this point, tells us nothing more than what is obvious: we die once, and then begins the whole business of "judgment," whatever that may entail for every soul.

The Bible does not oblige us to think either that this work of grace halts in its tracks when physical death occurs or that it is suddenly rushed to miraculous completion. . . . We deny death as an ultimate barrier (Howard, 124).

The vast majority of Protestants, however, do not and will not accept the practice of praying for the dead, because they do not see that it is supported in the New Testament (and *sola Scriptura* pretty much requires every doctrine to be explicitly taught in Holy Scripture). 2 Timothy 1:16-18 offers a possible instance of a prayer for the dead in the New Testament and, as such, is quite similar to 1 Corinthians 15:29. But Protestant commentators have been hopelessly confused about it and cannot offer a coherent, unified testimony as to its meaning.

Catholics agree with Protestants that some passages are more difficult to exegete than others, even considerably so. But we maintain that the primary reason for Protestant confusion with regard to certain "Catholic-sounding" texts (such as those dealt with in this book) is that they ignore one straightforward reading (in this case, that Paul is praying for a dead person) because such a viewpoint is not *allowed* within Protestantism; it is outside acceptable parameters.

It follows, then, that if any Bible passage teaches this or any doctrine that Protestants have long since rejected, it will be a mystery to Protestant commentators, and their interpretations are bound to contradict, as alternatives to the truth always do.

This passage offers another classic, prime example. The well-known Evangelical Protestant work *The New Bible Commentary*

(Guthrie, 1178; commentary by Guthrie himself) takes the astounding position that Onesiphorus is probably dead (citing 2 Tim. 4:19), yet holds that Paul was praying for his conduct during life; thus avoiding any implication of prayer for the dead. One might say that this is a distinction without a difference.

Jamieson, Fausset, and Brown also hold that Paul was praying, but obviously not for a dead man because, after all, "nowhere has Paul prayers for the dead, which is fatal to the theory . . . that he was dead." Well-known commentators Johannes Bengel (Lutheran: 1687-1752) and Henry Alford (Anglican: 1810-1871) thought he was dead (as mentioned by Jamieson, Fausset, and Brown in their commentary on the verse).

Greek scholar A. T. Robertson states, "Apparently Onesiphorus is now dead as implied by the wish in 1:18" (Robertson, IV, 615). He (somewhat amusingly) tries to save himself from the "Catholic" implications by referring to Paul's prayer as a "wish." The only possible difference I can see between "I *pray* that God will bless you" and "I *wish* that God will bless you" is that one could make a merely idle wish, whereas to pray invokes God's power thus and the real possibility that he will act and answer the prayer. But in both cases, the person is expressing his desire and hope.

St. Paul refers to the "household of Onesiphorus" twice (here and in 2 Tim. 4:19). This language leads some commentators to think he was dead (presuming that, if he were alive, Paul would have addressed him in the first person). For example, *The International Standard Bible Encyclopedia* states:

> It is not clear whether Onesiphorus was living, or whether he had died, before Paul wrote the epistle. Different opinions have been held on the subject. The way in which Paul refers to "the household . . . of Onesiphorus," makes it possible that Onesiphorus himself had died . . . but certainty is impossible.

But the author of this article, John Rutherford, plays word games as Robertson does, in another example of Protestant dogmatic overkill and bias adversely affecting exegesis, stating that if Onesiphorus was indeed dead:

> [T]he apostle's words in regard to him would be a *pious wish*, which has nothing in common with the abuses which have gathered around the subject of prayers for the dead, a practice which has no foundation in Scripture (Orr, IV, 2195; emphasis added).

What is a "pious wish"? I submit that if it is not prayer, it is close enough to the practice of prayer as to be indistinguishable from it, for all practical purposes, and that we are again observing a straining at gnats, borne of desperate exegesis, seeking to avoid at all costs any "Catholic" implications.

Protestant commentators Clarke, Henry, and Barnes, all appeal to desperate measures in their commentary on this passage. Clarke reduces the ostensible prayer to a mere "Hebraism," while Henry and Barnes casually assume (by circular reasoning; assuming what they are trying to prove) that Onesiphorus was not dead:

> Some think that this is a prayer to God the Father to communicate grace to him, that he might find mercy in the great day at the hand of Jesus Christ the Judge. It is probably only a Hebraism, for God grant that he may here be so saved by Divine grace, that in the great day he may receive the mercy of the Lord Jesus Christ unto eternal life.

Henry gets in his obligatory shot at the "papists":

> Though the papists will have it that he was now dead; and, from Paul's praying for him that he might find mercy, they conclude the warrantableness of praying for the dead; but who told them that Onesiphorus was dead?

Barnes writes similarly:

This proves that Onesiphorus was then alive, as Paul would not offer prayer for him if he were dead. The Papists, indeed, argue from this in favor of praying for the dead — assuming from 2 Timothy 4:19 that Onesiphorus was then dead. But there is no evidence of that.

To summarize this somewhat amusing confusion and catalog of evasive and rationalizing techniques, and what to do when faced with a Bible text utterly at odds with one's own theology, I offer the following chart:

Commentator	Was Onesiphorus dead?	Did Paul pray for Him?
New Bible Commentary	Possibly	Yes
Jamieson, Fausset, Brown	No	Yes
A. T. Robertson	"Apparently"	"Wishing"
International Standard Bible Encyclopedia	Possibly	"Pious wish"
The New Bible Dictionary	No position	Yes
Adam Clarke	No position	Maybe
Matthew Henry	Probably not	Yes
Albert Barnes	No	Yes
John Calvin	No	Yes

The tally of nine prominent examples is as follows: "apparently dead" (one), "possibly dead" (two), agnostic position (two), "probably not dead" (one), and "not dead" (three). That's about even, depending on how one grades the undecided votes. As for whether Paul prayed, that is less uncertain: "yes" votes (six), "maybe" (one), and description of his sentiments as "wishing" (two).

On the question of how possible or likely it is that Paul prayed for the dead, three rule it out altogether, holding that Onesiphorus was alive; two do not state whether they believe he was alive, so we cannot determine their position; one allows a distinct possibility, another, a slight one, and two admit some possibility, depending on whether one construes "wishing" as synonymous or similar to prayer.

All this confusion and disagreement suggests that Protestants really have no coherent explanation of this passage and that (quite possibly, given the oft-evidenced hostility to Catholicism in these same writers) the desperation and strained nature of much of this interpretation is indicative of their attempts to avoid arriving at conclusions harmonious with Catholic theology.

PRAYERS FOR THE DEAD
WHEN THE DEAD ARE RAISED

Acts 9:36-37, 40-41: "Now there was at Joppa a disciple named Tabitha, which means Dorcas. . . . In those days she fell sick and died. . . . But Peter . . . knelt down and prayed; then turning to the body he said, 'Tabitha, rise.' And she opened her eyes, and when she saw Peter she sat up. And he gave her his hand and lifted her up. Then calling the saints and widows he presented her alive."

This passage — in relation to prayers for the dead, which Catholics accept and Protestants deny — was suggested to me by my wife, Judy, as I was writing the preceding section. It had never occurred to me; I do not recall ever hearing such an argument made, and I was quite excited at the apologetic possibilities contained in this passage.

I readily grant that the example is unusual, because of the uniqueness of praying to raise someone from the dead (as distinguished from a prayer that aids someone in purgatory), and I agree that the Apostles had extraordinary powers of healing, so that this is not exactly a normative state of affairs, although even great miracles like these have occurred through the years.

Nevertheless, it seems indisputable that here St. Peter literally prayed for a dead person, as far as that goes — which Protestants say is not permitted by, and supposedly not recorded in, the Bible.

Furthermore, we have another familiar example of the same thing: Jesus praying for Lazarus, just before he was raised by the Lord: "Father, I thank thee that thou hast heard me. I knew that thou hearest me always, but I have said this on account of the people standing by, that they may believe that thou didst send me" (John 11:41-42). There is no recorded prayer at the raising of Jairus's daughter (Mark 5:35-43).

Protestants would no doubt argue in reply that this was the Lord Jesus and an even more unique case; but we are commanded to *imitate* him (including in prayer; for example, the Lord's Prayer), and it remains an example of prayer for the dead. The Bible informs us that the disciples raised people from the dead (Matt. 11:5; Luke 7:22) and that Jesus told them that they would be able to, and should, do so (Matt. 10:8). So they went out and did it, presumably with the use of prayer for that end. Thus, they prayed for the dead.

John Calvin challenged Catholics concerning prayers for the dead: "I ask them, in turn, by what word of God, by what revelation, by what example, is this done?" (in McNeill, *Institutes*, III, 5, 10). I have just offered two examples recorded in two Bible passages (in addition to Onesiphorus).

If dead saints are not too far "out of reach" to be prayed for and raised from the dead back to earthly life, then I submit that they are not too distant for us to pray for their souls while in purgatory (assuming — as Catholics do on several biblical grounds — that there is such a thing). As Jesus would ask the Pharisees, "Which of these two things is more difficult to do?" Matthew Henry comments:

In his healing [Aeneas] there was an implied prayer [Acts 9:32-35], but in this greater work he addressed himself to God by solemn prayer, as Christ when he raised Lazarus.

There we have it. It is inescapable logic:

1. Peter prayed for Tabitha and Jesus for Lazarus, that they be raised from the dead.

2. In order for such a miracle to occur, the person prayed for must be dead, by definition.

3. Therefore, Jesus and Peter both prayed for the dead, meaning such a thing is recorded in the written Word of God.

John Calvin in his *Commentaries* writes at length about St. Peter's prayer (later stating that he also "speaketh unto a corpse"), citing a precedent (Aeneas, from the preceding context of Acts 9:32-35):

When he healed Aeneas he brake out into these words, without making any stop, "Aeneas, Jesus Christ make thee whole."

Calvin later directed the reader to yet another biblical account of prayers for the dead: that of Elijah, as recorded in 1 Kings 17:17-24: "Then he stretched himself upon the child three times, and cried to the Lord, 'O Lord, my God, let this child's soul come into him again.' And the Lord hearkened to the voice of Elijah; and the soul of the child came into him again, and he revived" (17:21-22).

It is only fitting, then, that Calvin's query, "By what word of God, by what revelation, by what example, is this done?" should be answered by himself in another of his own works. We have only added the names of our Lord Jesus and St. Peter to the list of those who are shown praying for the dead in Holy Scripture, as confirmed by Protestant commentators, who, despite all, are convinced that no such thing exists in Scripture.

Furthermore, these acts would probably not have occurred *but* for the prayers. God has power over life and death and is entirely sovereign, but he involves human beings and incorporates their prayers into his providence. None of these people came back to life until they were prayed for.

Thus it is God's will and an entirely scriptural practice to pray for the dead. If it were not God's will for men to pray for such things, he would not have honored the prayer, and the dead person would not have been raised (1 John 5:14-15). Therefore, to rule out this practice is impossible, if we are to be true to the Bible.

The "line" between heaven and earth, or the afterlife (including purgatory) and earth, is not so rigid and absolute as many seem to assume. This was shown in my previous mention of dead saints who came back to earth (Moses and Elijah at the Transfiguration, Samuel, the two "witnesses" of Revelation, and the many people who came out of their tombs and walked around Jerusalem after Jesus' death). It is true that those events were a result of God's decree and not men's prayers, but nevertheless, they prove that the "line" is not absolute. Whatever God can and does do is proper for men to pray for.

That there exists a certain middle ground or intermediate state between salvation in heaven — never to be undone or reversed — and earthly existence, is a fact illustrated precisely by these instances of raising the dead. But under a strict Protestant eschatological interpretation, a person dies and is then immediately judged and granted eternal life in heaven or eternal damnation in hell. This conclusion is often bolstered by citing Hebrews 9:27: "It is appointed for men to die once, and after that comes judgment." It is assumed that judgment occurs not merely after death, but instantaneously upon death. But the text does not demand such an interpretation.

For instance, one could write, "It is appointed for men to graduate from high school once, and after that comes college." It need not even be soon after. One could also write, for example, "It is appointed for all Lutherans to be baptized once, and after that comes confirmation." Confirmation for Lutherans is indeed after baptism, but by some ten to twelve years in most cases.

So then, what of these four people who were dead and came back to life? Obviously, they were in some sort of intermediate state that was neither an earthly existence nor an irrevocable commencement of the state following judgment. The Protestant has no choice but to grant that much, even if these cases are deemed rare exceptions to the otherwise ironclad rule.

Therefore, in Scripture there *is* such a notion as an intermediate state, at least in some cases, however rare. This brings us back to an earlier point: if indeed it is possible for a person to be in this intermediate state and to be brought across the great line between life and death by prayer, then it seems equally plausible and possible by prayer to cause a person to advance in purgatory, following the principle laid down by Jesus when he said that it is easier to say "Your sins are forgiven" than to heal a man physically.

In other words, if we can pray and raise a dead body to life, and across the line from the afterlife to earthly life, we can also pray for the same person's soul in the afterlife. One is no more implausible or plausible than the other.

If Protestants demand biblical examples of praying for the dead, we have provided them. Even if they are exceptional cases, this is not fatal to the argument. All miracles are exceptions by definition. Raising the dead was certainly an exception to routine, humdrum everyday life, yet Jesus told his disciples to do it (Matt. 10:8).

If we can pray for a dead man to come back to life, it seems only likely that we can pray for his soul as well, since the first prayer presupposes an intermediate state wherein that soul (without a body) is neither in heaven nor hell, from which there is no end or exit (as far as it is revealed in Scripture).

If a person can be so aided in the *earthly* direction, why could he not be aided in the *heavenly* direction, and who can say whether there might be gradations or processes in the journey from earth to heaven?

Chapter Thirteen

The Blessed Virgin Mary

FULL OF GRACE: THE BLESSED VIRGIN MARY'S SINLESSNESS AND IMMACULATE CONCEPTION

Luke 1:28: "And he came to her and said, 'Hail, O favored one, the Lord is with you!' "[4]

Catholics believe that this verse is an indication of the sinlessness of Mary — itself the kernel of the more developed doctrine of the Immaculate Conception. But that is not apparent at first glance (especially if the verse is translated "highly favored," which does not bring to mind sinlessness in present-day language). I have done a great deal of exegesis and analysis of this verse, in dialogue with Evangelical Protestants, and so I shall draw from that thought and experience in this chapter.

Protestants are hostile to the notions of Mary's freedom from actual sin and her Immaculate Conception (in which God freed her from original sin from the moment of her conception) because they feel that this makes her a sort of goddess and improperly set apart from the rest of humanity. They do not believe that it was

---

[4] The RSVCE translates *kecharitomene* ("favored one" above) as "full of grace."

fitting for God to set her apart in such a manner, even for the purpose of being the Mother of Jesus Christ.

The great Baptist Greek scholar A. T. Robertson exhibits a Protestant perspective, but is objective and fair-minded, in commenting on this verse as follows:

> "Highly favored" (*kecharitomene*). Perfect passive participle of *charitoo* and means endowed with grace (*charis*), enriched with grace as in Ephesians. 1:6. . . . The Vulgate *gratiae plena* "is right, if it means 'full of grace *which thou hast received*; wrong, if it means 'full of grace *which thou hast to bestow*' " (Plummer; Robertson, II, 13).

Kecharitomene has to do with God's grace, as it is derived from the Greek root *charis* (literally, "grace"). Thus, in the KJV, *charis* is translated "grace" 129 out of the 150 times that it appears. Greek scholar Marvin Vincent noted that even Wycliffe and Tyndale (no enthusiastic supporters of the Catholic Church) both rendered *kecharitomene* in Luke 1:28 as "full of grace" and that the literal meaning was "endued with grace" (Vincent, I, 259).

Likewise, well-known Protestant linguist W. E. Vine defines it as "to endue with Divine favor or grace" (Vine, II, 171). All these men are Protestants (except Wycliffe, who probably *would* have been, had he lived in the sixteenth century or after it), and so cannot be accused of Catholic translation bias. Even a severe critic of Catholicism like James White cannot avoid the fact that *kecharitomene* (however translated) cannot be divorced from the notion of grace, and stated that the term referred to "divine favor, that is, God's grace" (White, 201).

Of course, Catholics agree that Mary has *received* grace. This is assumed in the doctrine of the Immaculate Conception: it was a grace from God which could not *possibly* have had anything to do with Mary's personal merit, since it was granted by God at the moment of her conception, to preserve her from original sin (as appropriate for the one who would bear God Incarnate in her very body).

The Catholic argument hinges on the meaning of *kecharitomene*. For Mary this signifies a *state* granted to her, in which she enjoys an extraordinary fullness of grace. *Charis* often refers to a power or ability that God grants in order to overcome sin (and this is how we interpret Luke 1:28). This sense is a biblical one, as Greek scholar Gerhard Kittel points out:

> Grace is the basis of justification and is also manifested in it ([Rom.] 5:20-21). Hence grace is in some sense a state (5:2), although one is always called into it (Gal. 1:6), and it is always a gift on which one has no claim. Grace is sufficient (1 Cor. 1:29). . . . The work of grace in overcoming sin displays its power (Rom. 5:20-21) (Kittel, 1304-1305).

Protestant linguist W. E. Vine concurs that *charis* can mean "a state of grace, e.g., Rom. 5:2; 1 Pet. 5:12; 2 Pet. 3:18" (Vine, II, 170). One can construct a strong biblical argument from analogy for Mary's sinlessness. For St. Paul, grace *(charis)* is the antithesis and "conqueror" of sin (emphases added in the following verses):

> **Romans 6:14:** "For *sin* will have no dominion over you, since you are not under law but under *grace*" (cf. Rom. 5:17, 20-21; 2 Cor. 1:12; 2 Tim. 1:9).

We are saved by grace, and grace alone:

> **Ephesians 2:8-10:** "For by *grace* you have been *saved* through faith; and this is not your own doing, it is the *gift* of God — *not because of works*, lest any man should boast. For we are his workmanship, created in Christ Jesus for good works, which God prepared beforehand, that we should walk in them" (cf. Acts

15:11; Rom. 3:24, 11:5; Eph. 2:5; Titus 2:11, 3:7; 1
Pet. 1:10).

Thus, the biblical argument outlined above proceeds as follows:

1. Grace saves us.

2. Grace gives us the power to be holy and righteous and without sin.

Therefore, for a person to be *full of grace* is both to be saved and to be completely, exceptionally holy. It is a "zero-sum game": the more grace one has, the less sin. One might look at grace as water, and sin as the air in an empty glass (us). When you pour in the water (grace), the sin (air) is displaced. A full glass of water, therefore, contains no air (see also, similar zero-sum-game concepts in 1 John 1:7, 9; 3:6, 9; 5:18). To be full of grace is to be devoid of sin. Thus we might reapply the above two propositions:

1. To be full of the grace that saves is surely to be saved.

2. To be full of the grace that gives us the power to be holy, righteous, and without sin is to be fully without sin, by that same grace.

A deductive, biblical argument for the Immaculate Conception, with premises derived directly from Scripture, might look like this:

1. The Bible teaches that we are saved by God's grace.

2. To be "full of" God's grace, then, is to be saved.

3. Therefore, Mary is saved (Luke 1:28).

4. The Bible teaches that we need God's grace to live a holy life, free from sin.

5. To be "full of" God's grace is thus to be so holy that one is sinless.

6. Therefore, Mary is holy and sinless.

7. The essence of the Immaculate Conception is sinlessness.

8. Therefore, the Immaculate Conception, in its essence, can be directly deduced from Scripture.

The only way out of the logic would be to deny one of the two premises, and hold either that grace does not save or that grace is not that power which enables one to be sinless and holy. It is highly unlikely that any Evangelical Protestant would take such a position, so the argument is a very strong one, because it proceeds upon their own premises.

In this fashion, the essence of the Immaculate Conception (i.e., the sinlessness of Mary) is proven from biblical principles and doctrines accepted by every orthodox Protestant. Certainly all mainstream Christians agree that grace is required both for salvation and to overcome sin. So in a sense my argument is only one of degree, deduced (almost by common sense, I would say) from notions that all Christians hold in common.

One possible quibble might be about *when* God applied this grace to Mary. We know (from Luke 1:28) that she had it as a young woman, at the Annunciation. Catholics believe that God gave her the grace at her conception so that she might avoid the original sin that she otherwise *would* have inherited, being human. Therefore, by God's preventive grace, she was saved from falling into the pit of sin, rather than rescued after she had fallen in.

All of this follows straightforwardly from Luke 1:28 and the (primarily Pauline) exegesis of *charis* elsewhere in the New Testament. It would be strange for Protestants to underplay grace, when they are known for their constant emphasis on grace alone for salvation. (We Catholics fully agree with that; we merely deny the tenet of "faith alone," as contrary to the clear teaching St. James and St. Paul.)

Protestants keep objecting that these Catholic beliefs are speculative; that is, that they go far beyond the biblical evidence. But once one delves deeply enough into Scripture and the meanings of the words of Scripture, they are not that speculative at all. Rather, it looks much more like Protestant theology has selectively trumpeted the power of grace when it applies to all the rest of us Christian believers, but downplayed it when it applies to the Blessed Virgin Mary.

What we have, then, is not so much a matter of Catholics reading into Scripture, as Protestants, in effect, reading certain passages *out of* Scripture altogether (i.e., ignoring their strong implications), because they do not fit in with their preconceived notions (yet another instance of my general theme).

My first online-debate opponent could not refute this reasoning in any effective way. He tried to produce some counter-verses, but they did not overcome the logic and force of the argument. Several other Protestants who had been following the dialogue then took up the challenge. Let us look at their responses:

First, it was argued that St. Stephen was also described as "full of grace" in Acts 6:8. But in that verse, the phrase is *pleres charitos*, not *kecharitomene*. If the Greek terminology is different, the argument loses most or all of its relevance and force.

The second argument was from Eric Svendsen, a Protestant apologist who specializes in opposing the Catholic Church. In one of his books, he states that the root word for *kecharitomene*, *charitoo*, is found elsewhere in Scripture (in the same participial form as in Luke 1:28); therefore, Catholics should consistently regard others to whom it is applied as sinless also:

> [C]haritoo . . . occurs in the same participial form in Sir. 18:17 with no theological significance. It also occurs in Eph. 1:6 where it is applied to all believers. . . . Are we to conclude on this basis that all believers are without original sin? (Svendsen, 129).

Ephesians 1:5-6 reads, "He destined us in love to be his sons through Jesus Christ, according to the purpose of his will, to the praise of his glorious grace which he freely bestowed on us in the Beloved."

Svendsen thinks this defeats the Catholic exegesis at Luke 1:28, but the variant of *charitoo* (grace) here is different *(echaritosen)*. According to Marvin Vincent, a well-known Protestant linguist and expert on biblical Greek, the meaning is:

> . . . not "endued us with grace," nor "made us worthy of love," but, as "grace — which he freely bestowed" (Vincent, III, 365).

Vincent indicates different meanings for the word *grace* in Luke 1:28 and Ephesians 1:6. He holds to "endued with grace" as the meaning in Luke 1:28, so he expressly contrasts the meaning here with that passage. A. T. Robertson defines the word in the same fashion, as "he freely bestowed" (Robertson, IV, 518).

As for the grace bestowed here on all believers being parallel to the fullness of grace bestowed upon the Blessed Virgin Mary, this simply cannot logically be the case, once proper exegesis is undertaken. Apart from the different meanings of the specific word used, as shown, grace is possessed in different measure by different believers, as seen elsewhere in Scripture:

> **2 Peter 3:18:** "But grow in the grace and knowledge of our Lord and Savior Jesus Christ. To him be the glory both now and to the day of eternity. Amen."

> **Ephesians 4:7:** "But grace was given to each of us according to the measure of Christ's gift" (cf. Acts 4:33; Rom. 5:20, 6:1; James 4:6; 1 Pet. 5:5; 2 Pet. 1:2).

The "freely bestowed" grace of Ephesians 1:6, then, cannot possibly be considered the equivalent of that "fullness of grace" applied to Mary in Luke 1:28 because it refers to a huge group of people, with different gifts and various levels of grace bestowed, as the verses just cited show. Svendsen's argument is as fallacious as the following analogy:

Suppose a group of Christian baseball players — some of the greatest and the least talented alike — prayed to God before a game:

"He destined us in love to be his ballplayers through Jesus Christ, according to the purpose of his will, to the praise of his glorious gift of athletic ability and talents which he freely bestowed on us in the Beloved."

Obviously, God granted the talents and abilities of each ballplayer, in the sense of being Creator and source of all good things. But are these talents given in equal measure? Of course not (see especially Eph. 4:7). Likewise, grace is given in different measure to believers. Therefore, Svendsen's argument that Ephesians 1:6 is a direct parallel to Luke 1:28 collapses. The mass of Christian believers as a whole possesses the same degree neither of grace nor of sanctity, and everyone knows this, from experience and revelation alike.

But Mary (as an individual person) was addressed in an extraordinary fashion by a title that, biblically, means the one so addressed is particularly exemplified by the characteristics of the title. Mary was "full of grace"; *kecharitomene* here takes on the significance of a noun. No attempt to downplay or diminish the significance of this will succeed. The meaning is all too clear.

Svendsen points out that Luke 1:28 uses the perfect tense, whereas Ephesians 1:6 does not, and that Catholics might use this argument to bolster their case (since that indicates a difference between the two passages). But he writes:

> [T]his does not help their case since the perfect tense speaks only of the current state of the subject without reference to how long the subject has been in that state, or will be in that state (Svendsen, 129).

So he tries to show by cross-referencing and Greek grammar that Luke 1:28 is neither unique nor a support for Mary's sinlessness or the Immaculate Conception. But the perfect stem of a Greek verb, denotes, according to Friedrich Blass and Albert DeBrunner, "continuance of a completed action" (*Greek Grammar of the New Testament* [Chicago: University of Chicago Press, 1961], 66). Mary, therefore, continues afterward to be full of the grace she possessed at the time of the Annunciation. That cannot, of course, be said of all believers in Ephesians 1:6, because of differences of levels of grace, as shown earlier.

As for Svendsen's cross-reference to Sirach 18:17, where the word is in the same form *(kecharitomene)* that verse also applies generally: "Indeed, does not a word surpass a good gift? Both are to be found in a gracious man."

Moreover, this is *proverbial*, or wisdom literature. According to standard hermeneutical principles, this is not the sort of biblical literature on which to build doctrines or systematic theology (or even precise meanings of words). The reason is that proverbial expression admits of many exceptions. For example, the statement "Happy people smile" may be true much of the time, but it is not always true. Proverbial language is, therefore, too imprecise to use in determining exact theological propositions. Meaning depends on context, as any lexicon will quickly prove.

Even apart from the important factor of the proverbial style of writing found in Sirach, linguists attribute different meanings to *kecharitomene* in the two verses. As Joseph Thayer, another great biblical Greek scholar, writes:

Luke 1:28: "to pursue with grace, compass with favor; to honor with blessings."
Sirach 18:17: "to make graceful, i.e., charming, lovely, agreeable" (Thayer, 667; Strong's word no. 5487).

Eric Svendsen's attempt to lump in Luke 1:28 with other "similar" passages has failed, because reputable linguists demonstrate that there are enough differences to cast doubt on his argument.

Context, grammar, and hermeneutical principles alike sink his case.

Most Protestant thinkers and opponents of Catholic doctrine would, I think, assume that the Immaculate Conception could easily be disproven from Scripture. But from an analysis of the verses cited, we see that, although it cannot be absolutely *proven* from Scripture alone, it cannot be ruled out on the basis of Scripture, either. What is more, a solid deductive and exegetical basis for belief in Mary's sinlessness, and thus her Immaculate Conception, *can* be drawn from Scripture alone.

Chapter Fourteen

Clerical Celibacy

VOLUNTARY EUNUCHS FOR THE
SAKE OF THE KINGDOM OF HEAVEN

Matthew 19:12: "For there are eunuchs who have been so from birth, and there are eunuchs who have been made eunuchs by men, and there are eunuchs who have made themselves eunuchs for the sake of the kingdom of heaven. He who is able to receive this, let him receive it."

The frequent argument of Protestants on the subject of clerical celibacy is that the Catholic Church makes a *requirement* out of something that Paul merely *recommends*. Catholics, so we are told, are guilty once again of smuggling in their "traditions of men" and an alleged animus against sexuality and marriage. When one of my Internet-dialogue opponents made this garden-variety point, I answered as follows:

I think you are straining at gnats. I had no problem with the Catholic requirement of celibacy for priests when I was a Protestant. Why do you, I wonder? Here we have a state of life that the apostle Paul argues is very spiritually beneficial, and so the Catholic Church makes it a requirement for its priests. What I see as biblical and practical wisdom, however, you regard as legalistic and "man-made." That truly amazes me. Would you also balk at the *requirement* of many denominations for four years of seminary training? After all, the Apostles didn't go to seminary, right? Why make it a requirement? It's not fair! If a pastor wants to remain theologically undereducated, no man or denomination has a right to force him to learn!

The debate continued: my opponent stated that Paul allowed for cases where celibacy would *not* apply. I replied: "Exactly. The gift is not given to all, lest the world population be reduced to zero in a hundred years or so." I was told that Paul made celibacy a "gift." I replied that the Catholic Church did also. He replied that it had to be given by God (that would obviously go along with the notion of its being a spiritual "gift"), as opposed to a "man-pronounced requirement." I countered:

Why, then, can't the Catholic Church (in the Western Latin Rites, that is, not all the Rites) draw its priests from among this pool who have felt so called and so gifted from God? How is that "man-made," when all we are doing is recognizing prior gifts from God? Every institution has the right to make whatever rules it deems necessary for its flourishing continuance.

The Catholic Church wants its priests to be as single-heartedly devoted to the Lord as they can be. Since Paul says that singleness is a means to that end (1 Cor. 7:32-35), we accept his wise counsel and select (in the Latin Rite) our priests from among the pool of those so called.

Some (most, of course) are called to marriage, and some few are called to celibacy. We choose our priests from the latter group. Thus, we are not hindering God or any individual in the least, but rather, cooperating with God's callings and purposes.

We have every right to draw our priests from this category of men, just as Protestants have a right to draw their pastors from those men who believe in *sola Scriptura* and *sola fide*. A spiritual institution can choose among those who have *already* been called to celibacy *by* God for its priests. There is nothing "forced," "unnatural," "unethical," "illogical," or "unbiblical" about that in the least.

The Trappists don't talk. So a blabbermouth obviously won't be called, or *feel* called, to become a Trappist monk! Any institution (not just a Christian body) can require any discipline that it sees as beneficial to itself, provided, of course, that such a rule is not immoral — and this certainly isn't.

Catholics are being very biblical in this view. Where in Protestantism is the calling of celibacy celebrated and honored, since it is strongly recommended by St. Paul and Jesus, and was the norm among the early Apostles, not to mention the early priests and bishops? We honor both celibacy and marriage. Protestants, however, seem to honor only the latter. They are just as legalistic as they claim we are by enforcing the "unwritten rule" that pastors ought always to be married.

In Catholic ascetic spirituality, or what are called "the evangelical counsels," a person may voluntarily (sometimes heroically) renounce something for the kingdom of God. That principle is even found in Protestantism to some extent (e.g., giving monetary donations to the point of sacrifice). It is certainly biblical (the prophets, John the Baptist, the disciples, and so forth).

There are many callings and roles to fill. Not everyone can be a Marine, or a Green Beret, or a Rhodes scholar, or an NBA all-star. Those are things that call for qualifications not everyone can meet (if you are five-foot-one, chances are you are not going to take up basketball; if you weigh 125 pounds, you will not be a linebacker in football). The priesthood is no different.

It is not by any means clear to me that a married clergy is a preferable or superior state of affairs. Most pastors end up forsaking time with their families, and are workaholics (as are many men). I even came up with a phrase for it: "Busy Pastor Syndrome." The wild, rebellious nature of "preacher's kids" is a well-known phenomenon in the Evangelical world. We used to call them "PKs." Even Billy Graham's son Franklin (who now has a wonderful and important ministry of his own) went through a very rebellious period.

I can see in my own life (as a full-time Catholic apologist and writer) that I have to balance carefully my vocation, my family life, my time alone with my wife, and my own leisure and relaxation. I cannot imagine having this family and shepherding a flock of so many hundred people. Being single in that situation makes all the sense in the world to me.

With this introduction to the topic, let us proceed to analyze how Protestant commentators approach the biblical texts that Catholics bring forth in support of their celibacy requirement for priests. John Calvin comments:

> [W]hat is their species of vows? They offer God a promise of perpetual virginity, as if they had previously made a compact with him to free them from the necessity of marriage. They cannot allege that they make this vow trusting entirely to the grace of God; for, seeing he declares this to be a special gift not given to all (Matt. 19:11[-12]), no man has a right to assume that the gift will be his. Let those who have it use it; and if at any time they feel the infirmity of the flesh, let them have recourse to the aid of him by whose power alone they can resist (*Institutes*, IV, 13, 17).

This is rather odd reasoning. Would anyone think this is a clear grappling with the biblical text? First, Calvin assumes that monks could not follow God's call by "trusting entirely" in his grace. How he knows this, we are not told. But in any event, it is obviously no argument; rather, merely a subtle form of personal attack against an entire class of people.

Then he denies that the calling to celibacy can be known with certainty because the gift is not for everyone. This is a highly interesting assertion indeed, that no one can be sure of his gift or calling from God. Whence does Calvin derive such knowledge? Certainly not from the Bible. How does he, then, assuming his desire to be logically consistent, possess certainty of his *own* calling? He has no problem, on the other hand, attributing inner certainty of a divine call for Protestant *pastors*. He casually assumes this, referring to:

> . . . that secret call of which every minister is conscious before God, but has not the Church as a witness of it; I mean, the good testimony of our heart. . . . This, as I have said, is indeed necessary for every one of us, if we would approve our ministry to God (*Institutes*, IV, 3, 11).

Yet when it comes to celibacy, all of a sudden Calvin arbitrarily changes his tune and concludes that "no man has a right to assume that the gift will be his." Jesus teaches us that it is possible; why does Calvin (and why do so many Protestants today) doubt it? Then he switches back again and says, "Let those who have it use it." We may be thankful, I suppose, that Calvin graciously allows them, despite his personal derision for the concept, to follow their consciences and the clear biblical warrant for such an estate ("each has his own special gift from God" — 1 Cor. 7:7).

In context it is clear that Calvin's objection is not biblically or rationally based, but stems from his hostility to the Catholic

Church, expressed in strident disapproval of its distinctives, such as clerical celibacy. (This seems to be a common tendency of the harshest critics of the Church.) He refers, for example, to monks who have forsaken their solemn vows for an "honest kind of livelihood," contrasted with those who "remained entangled in ignorance and error," and bound by "extraneous chains, which are nothing but the wily nets of Satan" and "superstition" (*Institutes*, IV, 13, 21).

Elsewhere, Calvin follows the pathetic example of Luther's many absurd and outrageous statements about the Catholic clergy:

> The sum of it all is that pope, devil, and his church hate the estate of matrimony, as Daniel says [17:37]; therefore he wants to bring it into such disgrace that a married man cannot fill a priest's office. That is as much as to say that marriage is harlotry, sin, impure, and rejected by God; and although they say, at the same time, that it is holy and a sacrament, that is a lie of their false hearts, for if they seriously considered it holy, and a sacrament, they would not forbid the priests to marry. Because they do forbid them, they must consider it unclean, and a sin, as they plainly say. . . .
>
> . . . [T]he noises made by monks and nuns and priests are not prayers or praises to God. They do not understand it and learn nothing from it; they do it like hard labor, for the belly's sake, and seek thereby no improvement of life, no progress in holiness, no doing of God's will (*On the Councils and the Churches*, 1539; in Jacobs, V, 284, 286).

Calvin, in other places, seems to admit the possibility of a divine calling to celibacy, but on a temporary basis only: "Virginity, I agree, is a virtue not to be despised. However, it is denied to some and granted to others only for a time" (in McNeill, *Institutes*, II, 8, 42). He gives no biblical rationale for this opinion; rather, he keeps prattling on in this section (he so often appears as if he is lecturing Catholics like small children in his *Institutes*) about the perfectly obvious: that celibacy is a gift from God and that no one can remain celibate without his power.

Calvin, then, has offered us nothing in the Bible to overthrow the Catholic position on clerical celibacy. His criticisms have left our view completely unaffected. And Luther's opinion has even strengthened it. Can the other classical Protestant commentators we have been examining produce a cogent, solid, biblical critique?

John Wesley sees in this verse the value of remaining single for the kingdom's sake, if one is *called* to it. Jamieson, Fausset, and Brown accept the obvious spiritual utility in the practice as well, and add, "Such was Paul." Adam Clarke thinks that the Lord was referring to the Essenes, who were celibate, and he shows no particular opposition to the idea. Albert Barnes thinks that this is a possibility also. Matthew Henry, too, understands the underlying principle.

So it looks as though Protestants cannot come up with any compelling or persuasive biblical argument against clerical celibacy, or any "un-Catholic" re-interpretation of Matthew 19:12. Many of the criticisms of celibacy made by Protestant opponents of the practice today are of the same nonbiblical, and usually emotionally based, nature.

"EACH HAS HIS OWN SPECIAL GIFT";
"UNDIVIDED DEVOTION TO THE LORD"

1 Corinthians 7:7-9: "I wish that all were as I myself am. But each has his own special gift from God, one of one kind and one of another. To the unmarried and the widows I say that it is well for them to remain single as I do. But if they cannot exercise self-control, they should marry. For it is better to marry than to be aflame with passion."

1 Corinthians 7:32-38: "I want you to be free from anxieties. The unmarried man is anxious about the affairs of the Lord, how to please the Lord; but the married man is anxious about worldly affairs, how to please his wife, and his interests are divided. And the unmarried woman or girl is anxious about the affairs of the Lord, how to be holy in body and spirit; but the married woman is anxious about worldly affairs, how to please her husband. I say this for your own benefit, not to lay any restraint upon you, but to promote good order and to secure your undivided devotion to the Lord. If anyone thinks that he is not behaving properly toward his betrothed, if his passions are strong, and it has to be, let him do as he wishes: let them marry — it is no sin. But whoever is firmly established in his heart, being under no necessity but having his desire under control, and has determined this in his heart, to keep her as his betrothed, he will do well. So that he who marries his betrothed does well; and he who refrains from marriage will do better."

St. Paul reiterates Jesus' teaching that it is good to be single in order to give undistracted devotion to the Lord, if a person is called to it. "Each has his own special gift from God," says Paul. If one is "aflame with passion," he is likely called to marry. Marriage is good; celibacy is better (if one is called to it). Marriage brings different responsibilities and problems. Paul is not anti-marriage; he is simply offering some fairly evident practical wisdom.

John Calvin keeps up his tirade against celibacy in his *Commentaries* (for 1 Cor. 7). He assumes that many Catholic clergy and religious have vowed celibacy without having the gift; and he assumes that many who do so despise marriage, that the very requirement produces all sorts of hideous and clandestine sexual sins, and that it is virtually impossible to live in a state of celibacy for very long:

> What, in the meantime, has been done? Every one, without having any regard to his *power*, has, according to his *liking*, vowed perpetual continency. . . . Virginity, I acknowledge, is an excellent gift; but keep it in view, that it is a *gift*. . . . As for those who, despising marriage, rashly vowed perpetual continency, God punished their presumption, first, by the secret flames of lust; and then afterwards, by horrible acts of filthiness. . . . [N]o house was safe from the impurities of the priests. Even that was reckoned a small matter; for there sprung up monstrous enormities. . . . We must also notice carefully the word *continue*; for it is possible for a person to live chastely in a state of celibacy for a time, but there must be in this matter no determination made for tomorrow.

Granted, Calvin was not writing during the most spiritually upright time in Church history, and it was right to respond to the scandals of sexual corruption in the priesthood, but that does not give him a warrant to disparage the biblical teaching and act as if celibacy is the root of all kinds of evil.

That is not what St. Paul teaches; that is not how the disciples lived their lives. Calvin would have it that Jesus require his closest companions and associates to live in a state that was almost certain to produce "the secret flames of lust" and "monstrous enormities." This is clearly absurd.

As with so many doctrines, here again is the early Protestant propensity for throwing out the baby with the bath water. If there was corruption or human failings, the Protestant solution was, too often, to throw out the institution rather than reform it. They claimed to be following the Bible in a special way that the

"papists" were not; yet on this issue they could produce no compelling proof that celibacy of priests ought to be abandoned.

They simply did not *like* the celibacy requirement, and so they
got rid of it. But Christian tradition does not work that way. The
Church is not at liberty to pick and choose or to discard received
traditions at whim. Celibacy was not dogma, but it was a very en-
trenched and successful practice in the Church. It is a disciplinary
requirement that can change and has changed in Church history.
We believe that it allows Catholic priests and religious to be closer
to St. Paul's ideal for "undistracted devotion to the Lord."

The general thrust of Calvin's long comment on 1 Corinthians
7 is to downplay every instance of St. Paul's praising celibacy and
to emphasize to the greatest degree lust and the supposed universal
requirement for marriage. He is, therefore, eisegeting, because his
concern is precisely the opposite of St. Paul's: to disparage celibacy
or virginity in practice as impossible and too easily overcome by
the lusts of the flesh.

The Catholic Encyclopedia, in its article on celibacy, gives the
counterargument to this way of thinking:

> [T]he observance of continence with substantial fidelity by
> a numerous clergy, even for centuries together, is assuredly
> not beyond the strength of human nature when elevated by
> prayer and strengthened by Divine grace. . . .
>
> Our argument is that the observance of celibacy is not
> only possible for the few called to be monks and enjoying
> the safeguards of the monastic life, but that it is not beyond
> the strength of a great body of men numbered by tens of
> thousands. . . . [S]candals are no more the effect of compul-
> sory celibacy than prostitution, which is everywhere ram-
> pant in our great cities, is the effect of our marriage laws.
>
> We do not abolish Christian marriage because so large a
> proportion of mankind are not faithful to the restraints

which it imposes on human concupiscence. . . . Neither is there any reason to suppose that scandals would be fewer and the clergy more respected if Catholic priests were permitted to marry (Herbermann, III, 483).

John Henry Newman (in words that are just as relevant to the situation of today's tragic sexual scandals) compared celibate and married clergy in terms of virtue, and contended that neither state is the cause of sinful behavior:

> I am very skeptical indeed that in matter of fact a married clergy *is* adorned, in any special and singular way, with the grace of purity. . . . I deny that they succeed with their rule of matrimony, better than we do with our rule of celibacy. . . . [A] Protestant rector or a dissenting preacher is not necessarily kept from the sins I am speaking of, because he happens to be married. . . .
>
> [T]here are, to say the least, as many offenses against the marriage vow among Protestant ministers, as there are against the vow of celibacy among Catholic priests. . . .
>
> It is not what the Catholic Church imposes, but what human nature prompts, which leads any portion of her ecclesiastics into sin. Human nature will break out, like some wild and raging element, under any system. . . . It is the world, the flesh, and the devil, not celibacy, which is the ruin of those who fall (*Lectures on the Present Position of Catholics in England*, Lecture 4, 134-136).[5]

---

[5] As for the recent, widely publicized sexual scandals in the Catholic Church, there is no evidence that priestly celibacy is one of its root causes. We know from research and crime statistics that child molesters come just as often from among married and sexually active men as from single or (presumed) celibate men (indeed, many instances of this monstrous sin occur in families, with fathers or mothers abusing their own children).

But returning to 1 Corinthians 7: Adam Clarke somehow manages to flip the Apostle Paul's meaning completely, with an astonishing contempt for the actual text he is supposedly expounding. St. Paul writes in 7:32-33: "The unmarried man is anxious about the affairs of the Lord, how to please the Lord; but the married man is anxious about worldly affairs, how to please his wife." But by some unknown, inexplicable process of reasoning from that text, Clarke can make this comment:

> The single man lives for and does good to himself only; the married man lives both for himself and the public. Both the state and the Church of Christ are dependent on the married man. . . . The married man, therefore, far from being in a state of inferiority to the single man . . . can do all the good the other can do, though perhaps sometimes in a different way; and he can do ten thousand goods that the other cannot possibly do. And therefore both himself and his state are to be preferred infinitely before those of the other.

All this flows from Clarke's assumption that Paul is only talking this way because of the "present distress"; otherwise he would prefer marriage to singleness. When he comments on verse 35, where Paul makes his strongest endorsement of the practical and spiritual benefits of celibacy over against marriage, he tries to evade the clear, straightforward meaning of the text: "Nothing spoken here was ever designed to be of general application; it

Furthermore, statistics for child molestation among Protestant married clergy are not all that different from the rates among Catholic priests. The scandal is horrible, tragic, and outrageous, and quite troubling in all its implications, but it is not, in and of itself, a reason to cast aspersions on the celibacy requirement. It is, rather, a wake-up call to screen potential priests far more closely than they have been in the past.

concerned the Church at Corinth alone, or Churches in similar circumstances."

Matthew Henry cannot refrain from the temptation to bash Catholic priestly vows irrationally. He acts, according to the general Protestant tendency, as if celibacy is nearly impossible, or as if it is forced upon Catholic clergy:

> [H]e would not lay celibacy on them as a yoke, nor, by seeming to urge it too far, draw them into any snare; and therefore says, *But I spare you*. Note how opposite in this are the papist casuists to the apostle Paul! They forbid many to marry, and entangle them with vows of celibacy, whether they can bear the yoke or no.

This is an utterly ridiculous remark. It calls to mind an imaginary Catholic Church where potential priests are dragged screaming and kicking (perhaps drugged up, too, and pulled from the arms of hysterical, grieving girlfriends) and forced to take their vows under gunpoint "whether they can bear the yoke or no."

Henry speaks nothing of spiritual gifts, vocation, the voluntary nature of a discernment of the calling to the priesthood, or the graces of Holy Orders. Rather than show how Catholic teaching is wrong from biblical teaching, he takes the opportunity to rave and to present an entirely jaded picture of Catholic belief and practice.

In conclusion, I would like to cite some wise words of G. K. Chesterton, written fourteen years before he became a Catholic. The paradox he notes is marvelously ironic: the Catholic Church is simultaneously attacked for being too "pro-family" and too "pro-children" but also for supposedly being against marriage and sexuality (see the last two chapters, as the Church, we are told, stifles marital and sexual happiness in its puritanical views on divorce and contraception), due to its high regard for the celibate life devoted to the Lord in a total giving of self. Chesterton's point is that one need not choose; it is a false dilemma from the start:

It is true that the historic Church has at once emphasized celibacy and emphasized the family; has at once (if one may put it so) been fiercely for having children and fiercely for not having children. It has kept them side by side like two strong colors, red and white. . . . [T]he whole theory of the Church on virginity might be symbolized in the statement that white is a color: not merely the absence of a color. All that I am urging here can be expressed by saying that Christianity sought in most of these cases to keep two colors coexistent but pure. It is not a mixture like russet or purple; it is rather like a shot silk, for a shot silk is always at right angles, and is in the pattern of the cross (Chesterton, 97).

Chapter Fifteen

Divorce

OUR LORD JESUS' "STRICT" STANCE ON DIVORCE

Matthew 19:9: " 'And I say to you: whoever divorces his wife, except for unchastity, and marries another, commits adultery.' "

The Catholic teaching on this passage and on the question of marriage and divorce in general can be summarized as follows: a valid sacramental marriage is indissoluble; that is, it cannot be undone as long as both spouses are alive. According to Matthew 19:6, the spouses "are no longer two but one flesh. What therefore God has joined together, let not man put asunder."

Nearly all Protestant churches today, although typically frowning upon divorce, allow exceptions for adultery or abandonment or similarly serious marital difficulties. The traditional stigma of divorce has lessened greatly in Protestant circles just as it has in the secular culture, and divorce is permitted under more and more circumstances. This has been the general trend since World War II and even before; and today, divorce rates among Evangelical Protestants are virtually as high as that of the general public.

To understand the present disagreement between Catholics and Protestants on divorce, it is useful to examine the basis of the supposed loopholes or exception clauses found in Jesus' teaching on the subject. The Greek word for *unchastity* in Matthew 19:9 is *porneia*, which is defined in standard Greek lexicons and other Bible study aids as "unlawful sexual intercourse." Catholics hold that Jesus is here contrasting a true marriage with a state of concubinage or some other illicit union. If there is not truly a marriage present, then a separation can take place, but it is not truly a divorce, because there was no marriage there to begin with.

Many people use this verse, along with Matthew 5:32, to justify divorce based on the occurrence of adultery, yet the ordinary Greek word for *adultery (moicheia)* is not used. This supports the Catholic case that Jesus is referring to something else, for if adultery was the plain intent and meaning (the passage being about marriage in the first place), surely *moicheia* would have been used, as it is in many other places (thirty-five times in one of its forms).

The Greek word *porneia* and its cognates are never translated in the KJV New Testament as "adultery" but as "fornication" or "fornicator" (thirty-nine times), "harlot" (eight times), "whore" (four), and "whoremonger" (five). Likewise, every variant of the English *fornication* in the KJV is always a translation of some form of *porneia*.

The same holds true for *adultery* and its variants, which always are translations of some form of *moicheia* (which, in turn, are never translated as anything other than "adultery"). We also see the two Greek words distinguished from each other in the same verse (Matt. 5:19; Mark 7:21; Gal. 5:19).

The opinion rendered in Gerhard Kittel's standard lexical work, in its comments on *moicheia* and its cognates, appears to be consistent with the "strict" Catholic interpretation of the biblical teaching on marriage and divorce:

Marriage is a lifelong partnership, divorce is contrary to God's original purpose (Matt. 19:6 ff.), and remarriage after divorce is adultery (Matt. 5:32, 19:9; Mark 10:11-12; Luke 16:18). . . . Paul upholds the teaching of Jesus in the lax Hellenistic world (1 Cor. 5:1 ff., 6:9) (Kittel, 606).

Kittel's comments on *porneia* are even more noteworthy:

As regards divorce, debate arises concerning Matt. 5:32 and 19:9. In Mark 10:9, 16:18; 1 Cor. 7:10 Jesus teaches the indissolubility of marriage as God's unconditional will. . . . The problem in Matt. 5:32 and 19:9 is perhaps that Jewish Christians who keep the law are required to divorce adulterous wives and hence cannot be responsible if these contract a new relationship which is from a Christian standpoint itself adulterous. Divorce itself is not conceded (Kittel, 920).

The International Standard Bible Encyclopedia also takes a very strict line (quite unpopular in many Evangelical circles today):

A question of profound interest remains to be treated: Did Jesus allow under any circumstances the remarriage of a divorced person during the lifetime of the partner to the marriage? Or did He allow absolute divorce for any cause whatsoever? . . . If we had only the Gospels of Mark and Luke and the Epp. of Paul, there could be but one answer given: Christ did not allow absolute divorce for any cause (see Mark 10:2 ff.; Luke 16:18; Gal. 1:12; 1 Cor. 7:10) (Orr, III, 1999).

The article then tries to explain the Matthean passages (note how they are deemed as seemingly contradictory, rather than complementary with Mark and Luke) by recourse to a theory of textual change:

Two sayings attributed to Christ and recorded by the writer or editor of the First Gospel (Matt. 5:32; 19:9) seem directly to

contravene His teaching as recorded in Mark and Luke. . . .
A critical examination of the whole passage in Matthew
has led many scholars to conclude that the exceptive clause
is an interpolation due to the Jewish-Christian compiler or
editor through whose hands the materials passed. Others
think it betrays traces of . . . literary revision and compila-
tion. . . . Certainly much is to be said for the view which is
steadily gaining ground, that the exception in Matthew is
an editorial addition made under the pressure of local conditions and practical necessity, the absolute rule being found
too hard (Orr, III, 1999).

It is very widely maintained in the Christian church that
there should be no divorce for any cause whatever (Orr, II,
866).

The author of this second article ("Divorce") argues that this
strict position (note how different things in Protestant circles
were in 1929, when the first edition of this work was published) is
contrary to Matthew 5:32 and 19:9, which, in his opinion, allow
for divorce and remarriage, but that Paul's teaching in 1 Corinthians 7:15 concerning desertion does not allow for divorce and remarriage of the innocent party, and that only once in the first
eight hundred years of the Church did anyone interpret Paul
differently:

That no use was ever made of such construction of Paul in
the whole era of the adjustment of Christianity with hea-
thenism is good evidence that it was never there to begin
with (Orr, II, 866).

Thus we see that the history of Christian teaching on divorce is
surprisingly strict by today's standards. Yet some Protestants, although they might believe that God sometimes speaks to them in-
dividually, refuse to consider what God may have been speaking to

the great mass of Christians over the past two thousand years. Catholics, however, believe that Christian history and historical exegesis and moral beliefs of Christians still *mean* something for us today.

Baptist Greek scholar A. T. Robertson also prominently mentioned the same textual theory in his comments on Matthew 19:9 and 5:32 (although he himself disagrees with it):

> Here, as in 5:31 ff., a group of scholars deny the genuineness of the exception given by Matthew alone. McNeile holds that "the addition of the saving clause is, in fact, opposed to the spirit of the whole context, and must have been made at a time when the practice of divorce for adultery had already grown up."
>
> McNeile denies that Jesus made this exception because Mark and Luke do not give it. He claims that the early Christians made the exception to meet a pressing need (Robertson, I, 155, 47).

The Oxford Dictionary of the Christian Church allows for more possibility that this was indeed the case:

> [T]he Lord . . . abrogated the Mosaic toleration of divorce (Matt. 5:31 f., 19:3-9; Mark 10:2-12; Luke 16:18) and condemned remarriage. The "Matthean exception" permitting remarriage (19:9), which conflicts with the other Gospels, the rest of the NT, and the general tradition of the Western Church, is perhaps to be understood as an early gloss to render the Christian law easier (Cross, 889).

To summarize this at-times confusing material: according to the several reputable Protestant reference sources surveyed here, a significant number of Bible scholars hold that Jesus' recorded teachings concerning divorce in Matthew contradict his teaching in Mark and Luke because of the "exception clause" in Matthew.

Some, therefore, have concluded that this clause was a later addition to the actual inspired biblical text. Also, some of these sources concede that the "strict interpretation" of St. Paul's teaching on divorce was held for the first eight hundred or so years of Church history.

One must be careful, if taking this textual approach, not to deny biblical infallibility and inspiration. If it can be demonstrated that a portion of the text was not actually in the Bible in the first place (an interpolation, or textual error, or text only in late manuscripts, such as Mark 16), then this poses no problem for inspiration. But if it is part of the Bible, it must be synthesized with the rest of the Bible in a harmonious whole, and cannot be contradictory.

The fascinating thing in the above citations is that the problem comes up at all. Obviously, people were concerned about an alleged contradiction or a vexing hermeneutical difficulty, because they thought it was so clear that Jesus and Paul did not allow exceptions, except in Matthew, where the text is then questioned as a later addition. In other words, the Bible is not so crystal clear and self-interpreting as Protestants are wont to believe. And perhaps the "strict" Catholic view concerning marriage and divorce is not as utterly unfounded as many are led to believe.

The eminent Protestant Bible scholar James Dunn goes further; in fact too far, if his position is that the apostle Matthew himself deliberately altered received Christian tradition: up to and including the very sayings of Jesus, and thus contradicted inspired Scripture elsewhere. This is unacceptable and must be deemed as an erosion of a high, inspired view of Holy Scripture; nevertheless, it is helpful to elucidate the controversy over how Matthew 19:9 can be harmonized with the other passages to arrive at a coherent viewpoint on marriage and divorce:

> Some sayings have been *interpreted differently* in the course of transmission. . . . We must note also how some sayings of

Jesus have been deliberately altered in the course of transmission — altered in such a way as to give a *clearly different* sense from the original. . . . Note also the way in which Jesus' clear-cut verdict against divorce preserved in Mark 10:11 has been softened by the addition of the unchastity clause in Matt. 19:9. . . .

[T]he unconditional ruling of Jesus in Mark 10.11 is amended by Matthew to allow the possibility of divorce in cases of unchastity (Dunn, 73-74, 247).

Moving from biblical teaching to the history of Christian teaching throughout the centuries, we find that the early Church took a very "strict" view of divorce and remarriage, which is a relevant consideration for the many Protestants who see themselves as hearkening back to the beliefs and practices of the early Christians. In his book about the first five centuries of the Church, *Early Christianity*, Protestant historian (and famous Luther biographer) Roland Bainton stated, "Second marriages were not permissible unless the first partner died prior to the baptism of the survivor" (p. 56).

The Catholic Encyclopedia provides an overview of Sacred Tradition on the question:

The testimonies of the Fathers and the councils leave us no room for doubt. In numerous places they lay down the teaching that not even in the case of adultery can the marriage bond be dissolved or the innocent party proceed to a new marriage. They insist rather that the innocent party must remain unmarried after the dismissal of the guilty one, and can only enter upon new marriage in case death intervenes (Herbermann, V, 56-57).

That article goes on to document this view from numerous patristic sources, including the *Shepherd of Hermas*, Justin Martyr,

The Catholic Verses

Athenagoras, Tertullian, Clement of Alexandria, Basil of Cæsarea, John Chrysostom, Theodoret, Ambrose, Jerome, and Augustine.

The leading magazine of Evangelical Protestantism, *Christianity Today* (founded by Billy Graham), confirms these beliefs of the early Church. Michael Gorman, in his article "Divorce and Remarriage from Augustine to Zwingli" (December 14, 1992) wrote:

> In the early church, many voices addressed the subjects of marriage, divorce, and remarriage, but their message, on the whole, was quite unified. Christian marriage, they said, is an indissoluble bond. Divorce, with the implicit right of remarriage, was not an option for Christian couples (though Origen admits some toleration existed), but permanent separation was. Remarriage after separation was considered punishable adultery or bigamy.

Luther and Calvin allowed divorce on a number of grounds, but historically many Protestant denominations and individuals have been stricter in their beliefs and practices concerning divorce. In Protestant churches today, however, there are ever more permissive attitudes toward divorce and remarriage. This goes far beyond the teaching of the Bible itself (even if one accepts an "adultery clause") and is another instance of the decay of biblical orthodoxy and traditional Christian morality among many Protestants.[6]

Christianity Today's issue of December 14, 1992 featured a survey of more than a thousand of its readers. Here is what it found with regard to views on remarriage:

[6] It must also be noted that individual Catholics have also fallen prey to the cultural watering down of strictly interpreted marriage vows and traditional Christian opposition to divorce, and statistically, they divorce at nearly the same rates as the rest of society. Official Catholic teaching on the indissolubility of marriage, however, has never wavered; furthermore statistics also show that *regular churchgoing* Catholics divorce at a much lower rate.

Seventy-three percent accept the remarriage of a Christian if the former spouse committed adultery or remarried. . . . Only 4 percent of the subscribers completely rule out any remarriage for a Christian after divorce.

The majority believe that fornication (73 percent) and desertion by a non-Christian spouse (64 percent) are two scriptural grounds for remarriage. At the same time, a significant minority believe Jesus taught that believers should not remarry after divorce (44 percent) and that God designed marriage to be permanent, and remarriage constitutes adultery (44 percent). Less than four out of ten believe there may be reason for remarriage other than adultery or desertion.

Christians — Catholics and Protestants alike — need to get back to the biblical teaching on marriage and divorce that was held by the early Church. One Protestant proponent of the early Church view is William A. Heth, professor of New Testament and Greek at Taylor University in Upland, Indiana, and coauthor with Gordon Wenham of *Jesus and Divorce* (Thomas Nelson). In that same issue of *Christianity Today*, in a piece entitled "Remarriage: Two Views," he debated another Protestant professor, and argued:

Even though marital separation or legal divorce may be advisable under some circumstances (persistent adultery, abuse, incest), Jesus calls remarriage after any divorce adultery. . . . [T]extual studies now confirm that the original text of both Matthew 19:9 and 5:32 contain Jesus' additional unqualified statement that finalizes his teaching on the subject: "And whoever marries a divorced woman commits adultery."

Paul's "let them remain unmarried or else be reconciled" (1 Cor. 7:10-11) says the same thing. . . . Where Paul specifically mentions the possibility of remarriage, in both instances he notes quite explicitly that one of the spouses has died (1 Cor. 7:39; Rom. 7:2-3).

Finally, in 1 Corinthians 7:27-28, Paul is not telling divorced individuals to feel free to remarry. He is telling engaged or formerly engaged couples who have come under the ascetic teaching at Corinth to feel free to marry should they so desire (see vv. 33-38).

Christians who are serious about conforming their lives to the commands of God in the inspired Bible need to ponder all of these things very carefully. It is not enough merely to coast along with the spirit of the times. St. Paul commands us to "not be conformed to this world but be transformed by the renewal of your mind, that you may prove what is the will of God, what is good and acceptable and perfect" (Rom. 12:2). The Catholic Church and more traditional Protestant churches that still disallow divorce can work together to try to influence our culture and to be "salt": to preserve it from further moral and familial decay.

Chapter Sixteen

Contraception

THE SIN OF ONAN

Genesis 38:9-10: "But Onan knew that the off-spring would not be his; so when he went in to his brother's wife he spilled the semen on the ground, lest he should give offspring to his brother. And what he did was displeasing in the sight of the Lord, and he slew him also."

Catholics believe that contraception is a gravely disordered violation of natural law, because it removes from sexuality its deepest purpose and function: procreation. To contracept involves a deliberate attempt to make conception not possible, or highly unlikely, while still enjoying the pleasures of sexuality. It attempts to tie God's hands, so to speak. But most Protestants today do not regard contraception as sinful at all, but simply as a morally neutral (or even obligatory) part of family planning.

Most Protestants (and Catholics for that matter) consider opposition to contraception a distinctively "Catholic thing" that has long been a point of division among Christian churches. Yet it is a matter of historical fact that *no* Christian communion sanctioned contraception until the Anglican Lambeth Conference in 1930.

Protestant historian Roland Bainton states casually that the Church "very early forbade contraception" (*Early Christianity*, 56). According to *The Oxford Dictionary of the Christian Church*, "many Christian moralists . . . repudiate all methods of family limitation" (Cross, 889). The great Catholic writer and convert Fr. Ronald Knox eloquently recounted how Christians used to detest contraception:

> Practices hitherto connected with the unmentioned underworld have found their way into the home. . . . [I]t is not merely a Christian principle that has been thrown overboard. . . . Ovid and Juvenal, with no flicker of Christian revelation to guide them, branded the practices in question with the protest of heathen satire. It is not Christian morality, but natural morality as hitherto conceived, that has been outraged by the change of standard (Knox, 31-32).

Christianity (Catholicism, Orthodoxy, and Protestantism alike) had always opposed contraception as gravely sinful, until just two generations ago. When I first learned of this in 1990 (as an inquiring Evangelical prolife activist very curious about the "odd" and inexplicable Catholic prohibition), it was a shocking revelation and the first step on my road to conversion to Catholicism.

Today, the great majority of Protestants and even of Catholics use contraceptives. It is a mortal sin in Catholicism, and used to be considered an extremely serious sin in Protestant circles (how things change!). C. S. Lewis, for example, opposed contraception:

> As regards contraceptives, there is a paradoxical, negative sense in which all possible future generations are the patients or subjects of a power wielded by those already alive. By contraception simply, they are denied existence; by contraception used as a means of selective breeding, they are, without their concurring voice, made to be what one

generation, for its own reasons, may choose to prefer. From this point of view, what we call Man's power over Nature turns out to be a power exercised by some men over other men with Nature as its instrument (*The Abolition of Man*, 68-69).

Genesis 38:9-10, about Onan, has been one of the main proof texts traditionally used to oppose contraception, as it would seem to be a description of *coitus interruptus*, a form of contraception. Traditionally, Protestants regarded this as an extremely serious sin and shameful act. Observe, for example, how Martin Luther passionately interpreted this biblical passage:

Onan must have been a malicious and incorrigible scoundrel. This is a most disgraceful sin. It is far more atrocious than incest and adultery. We call it unchastity, yes, a Sodomitic sin. For Onan goes in to her; that is, he lies with her and copulates, and when it comes to the point of insemination, spills the semen, lest the woman conceive. Surely at such a time the order of nature established by God in procreation should be followed. . . . He was inflamed with the basest spite and hatred. . . . Consequently, he deserved to be killed by God. He committed an evil deed. Therefore God punished him. . . . That worthless fellow . . . preferred polluting himself with a most disgraceful sin to raising up offspring for his brother (*Lectures on Genesis: Chapters 38-44*; 1544; LW, 7, 20-21).

Calvin, in his *Commentary on Genesis*, is no less vehemently opposed to the practice (what would he think if he knew about the vast majority of Calvinists today who regularly contracept?):

It is a horrible thing to pour out seed besides the intercourse of man and woman. Deliberately avoiding the intercourse, so that the seed drops on the ground, is doubly horrible. For this means that one quenches the hope of his family, and kills the son, which could be expected, before he is born. . . . Moreover he [Onan] thus has, as much as was in his power, tried to destroy a part of the human race. When a woman in some way drives away the seed out the womb, through aids, then this is rightly seen as an unforgivable crime.

The New Bible Dictionary concludes, on the other hand, "this verse does not pass any judgment on birth control as such" (Douglas, 789). The reasoning often used to overcome the force of the verse is to say that Onan was punished by God (with death) for disobeying the "levirate law," whereby a brother of a dead husband was to take his sister-in-law as his wife and have children with her (Deut. 25:5-10). The debate, then, is whether Onan was punished simply for disobeying the levirate law (regardless of how he did so), or more specifically for engaging in an act that was unnatural and immoral (so much so that God killed him as a result).

But we know that the violation of the levirate law cannot apply in this case (or any other) because the levirate law allowed the brother the option of refusing. Thus, we find in Deuteronomy 25:9 that a sister-in-law so refused should "spit in his face," but there is no mention of any death penalty or the wrath of God.

How then, can *The New Bible Dictionary* maintain that the slaying of Onan by God had no relation to contraception? God did not command Onan in this case — another argument sometimes heard — so he was not directly disobeying God; it was his father Judah who asked him to do what he did not want to do (Gen. 38:8). Whatever was displeasing to God could not have been disobedience of the levirate law, which is a crime not nearly as serious as being "wicked" — the reason God slew Onan's brother Er (Gen. 38:7).

Moreover, the passage that teaches about the levirate law (Deut. 25:5-10) is from God, as part of the covenant and the Law received by Moses on Mt. Sinai, and proclaimed by him to all of

Israel (see Deut. 5:1-5, 29:1,12). If God himself did not say that the punishment for disobeying the levirate law was death (in the place where it would be *expected* if it were true), how can modern commentators *know* that it was? Can it be that they are seeking to avoid uncomfortable implications of a biblical prohibition of contraception?

Yet *The New Bible Dictionary*'s article on Onan (the earlier comment was from the article "Marriage"), written by the editor, J. D. Douglas, states:

> Onan . . . took steps to avoid a full consummation of the union, thus displeasing the Lord, who slew him (Douglas, 910).

Douglas appears to contend that Onan was killed for the *contraceptive act*, not for disobedience to the levirate law. If so, his opinion contradicts the view expressed in the other article by J. S. Wright and J. A. Thompson. *The Eerdmans Bible Dictionary* concurs:

> [W]henever Onan and Tamar had intercourse he would spill his sperm on the ground to prevent her from conceiving; for this the Lord slew him.
>
> Onan's tactic of withdrawing before ejaculation . . . costs him his life (Myers, 781, 653).

In its article "Levirate Law," we are also informed that "the brother had the option of refusing to take his sister-in-law in levirate marriage" (Myers, 652). The logic is apparent: if refusal alone was not grounds to be killed by God or by capital punishment issued by his fellows, there must have been something in the *way* Onan refused that was the cause. This was the withdrawal method, a form of contraception (probably the one most used throughout history). Therefore, Onan was killed for doing *that*, which in turn means that God did not approve of it.

One might still retort as follows: "It is not contraception per se that was wrong in Onan's case, but the fact that he wanted to have sex with the woman but not to have children. He had the right to refuse the levirate marriage, but once he agreed to it he was obligated to produce the children, which was the *purpose* of it."

I would agree with this hypothetical objection *prima facie*, but I would add that it actually *confirms* the central moral point on which the moral objection to contraception is based: the evil of separating sex from procreation. It is precisely *because* the central purpose of marriage is procreation that the levirate law was present in the first place.

But Onan tried to separate sex from procreation. He wanted all the pleasure but not the responsibility of perpetuating his brother's family. He possessed the "contraceptive mentality" that is rampant today, even among otherwise traditional, committed Christians.

This is what is evil: an unnatural separation of what God intended to be together. Onan tried the "middle way" of having sex but willfully separating procreation from it. This was the sin, and this is why God killed him. Martin Luther understood the fundamental evil of contraception and the anti-child mindset:

> Today you find many people who do not want to have children. Moreover, this callousness and inhuman attitude, which is worse than barbarous, is met with chiefly among the nobility and princes, who often refrain from marriage for this one single reason, that they might have no offspring . . . [or] for fear that the members of their house would increase beyond a definite limit. Surely such men deserve that their memory be blotted out from the land of the living. Who is there who would not detest these swinish monsters? (*Lectures on Genesis: Chapters 1-5*, 1536; LW, I, 118; commentary on Genesis 2:18).

The rest of the populace is more wicked than even the heathen themselves. For most married people do not desire offspring. Indeed, they turn away from it and consider it better to live without children. . . . But the purpose of marriage is not to have pleasure and to be idle but to procreate and bring up children. . . . Those who have no love for children are swine, stocks, and logs unworthy of being called men and women; for they despise the blessing of God, the Creator and Author of marriage (*Lectures on Genesis: Chapters 26-30*; LW, V, 325-328; vol. 28, 279; commentary on the birth of Joseph to Jacob and Rachel; cf. LW, vol. 45, 39-40).

In summary, I would note the following aspects of the exegesis of the Onan passage:

1. The ancient and classical Jewish commentators thought the Onan passage condemned unnatural intercourse and masturbation.

2. If indeed God punished Onan merely for disobeying the levirate law (contrary to the penalty for such obedience, as recorded elsewhere), it is very odd that crude physical detail of what Onan did is included in the text. The Bible is always very restrained in its descriptions of marital intercourse. Explicit language is used, on the other hand, to refer to wicked and immoral sexual acts.

3. Jewish culture abhorred another form of "wasting the seed" — sodomy and homosexuality — even prescribing the death penalty for it.

4. If "wasting the seed" violates the natural law (see Rom. 1: 26-27; 2:14), this would account for Onan's act serving as an illustration in Scripture of a sin deserving severe punishment from God.

5. The virtually unanimous interpretation of the Onan passage in the same sense as Luther's and Calvin's commentary, by both Christian and Jewish commentators, is as striking as the universal consensus against contraception. For those who value the insights

of historical exegesis and Christian tradition, this cannot fail to be a relevant consideration in the discussion.

I believe that contraception is a "test case" today for how far Christians are willing to go to be countercultural and to live lives distinct from those of unbelievers. The sexual issues are always the ones where Christians are most in danger of compromise, because they are the most difficult to live out consistently. Yet both Scripture and the complete unanimity of Christian teaching against contraception until some seventy-five years ago provide a stern warning against such compromise, and a clear manifestation of God's moral commandments about sexuality and procreation.

Conclusion

It is my hope that examination of these "Catholic verses," and the Protestant critiques and Catholic countercritiques, has provided food for thought and further appreciation of Holy Scripture. The Bible is our common heritage, and if we approach it with an open mind, and an openness to the interpretations of historical Christianity, we can arrive at a fuller understanding of truth, grow in the Christian life, and become closer to God, the author of the Bible.

Errors in logic and theology and historical fact can be committed by commentators of any religious affiliation, and by otherwise intellectually brilliant and godly men and women. Catholics are often accused of ignoring the Bible, misinterpreting it, or adding corrupt "traditions of men" to it. I have tried to demonstrate that we are not unique in that respect, and that Catholics can turn the tables on such an argument. Catholics need not yield an inch when it comes to adherence to and respect for the Bible.

Protestantism may in many cases foster a high regard for the Bible and Bible study, but that does not make individual Protestants immune to the shortcomings of bias, eisegesis, faulty reasoning, or other flaws in methodology in doing biblical hermeneutics, commentary, and exegesis.

After all, in the highly charged, polemicized five-hundred-year "battle" between Protestants and Catholics, emotions run very high on both sides. In such a milieu, bias and lack of objectivity toward even the Bible, which both sides love and revere, is inevitable, and there are many knee-jerk reactions on both sides, as well as overreactions for fear of "sounding like" one's theological opponent.

We all would do well to examine whether our natural biases and party affiliations, which we all have, unduly affect our exegesis. We have nothing to lose from such reflection, and everything to gain. It is also true that even otherwise noble and respectable scholarly traditions often perpetuate various inherited biases, prejudices, and blind spots. These get passed down, and people forget that they are (surprisingly often) merely unproven assumptions that people no longer try to prove, but rather, simply accept as one of their own traditions (assuming that someone "important" has indeed proven them sometime in the past).

Just as we propose (perhaps a bit presumptuously) that the biblical passages examined in these pages are Catholic verses, so our Protestant friends would, no doubt, submit at least ninety-five verses of their own that they could consider the Protestant verses. Catholics need to be as eager and willing to grapple with those as we expect Protestants to deal with what we consider our proof texts and particularly strong supports of our system and theology.

I am more than happy to take on any such challenge in the course of my apologetic endeavors. And I urge other Catholic apologists and students of theology to exhibit the same willingness. I think serious joint Bible studies between Catholics and Protestants could yield some significant beneficial results and helpful insights (without either side compromising its heartfelt beliefs).

Again, it is my hope and devout wish that both sides (and also our Orthodox brethren) will be more eager to engage in discussion of the Bible with those of different persuasions. Such encounters should ideally be regarded as great opportunities to challenge one's own assumptions and conclusions, and — if nothing else — to sharpen one's own defenses of his beliefs, or to discard them if that is warranted.

In most cases, we will not change our opponents' minds in any significant way (or change our own), but at least greater understanding, charity, and mutual respect can be fostered among fellow disciples of our Lord Jesus Christ (Gal. 6:10).

Bibliography

Albright, William F. and C. S. Mann. *Anchor Bible: Matthew*. Garden City, New York: Doubleday, 1971.

Althaus, Paul. *The Theology of Martin Luther*. Translated by Robert C. Schultz. Philadelphia: Fortress Press, 1966.

Armstrong, John, ed. *Roman Catholicism: Evangelical Protestants Analyze What Divides and Unites Us*. Chicago: Moody Press, 1994.

Atkinson, James, ed. and trans. *Luther: Early Theological Works* (The Library of Christian Classics series). Philadelphia: Westminster Press, 1962.

Bainton, Roland H. *Early Christianity*. New York: D. Van Nostrand Company, 1960.

Bainton, Roland H. *Here I Stand*. New York: Mentor Books, 1950.

Barnes, Albert [Presbyterian]. *Barnes' Notes on the New Testament*. Grand Rapids, Michigan: Baker Book House, 1983. Available online: http://www.studylight.org/com/bnn/.

Berger, Peter L. *The Sacred Canopy*. Garden City, New York: Doubleday, 1967.

Berkouwer, G. C. *Faith and Justification: Studies in Dogmatics*. Translated by Lewis B. Smedes, Grand Rapids, Michigan: Eerdmans Pub. Co., 1954.

Blomberg, Craig L. *The New American Commentary: Matthew*. Volume 22. Nashville: Broadman, 1992.

Boice, James Montgomery, ed. *The Foundation of Biblical Authority*. Grand Rapids, Michigan: Zondervan, 1978. Chapter four by R. C. Sproul: "*Sola Scriptura*: Crucial to Evangelicalism."

Bonnet, Jules, ed. John Calvin: *Selected Works of John Calvin: Tracts and Letters: Letters, Part 2, 1545-1553*, volume 5 of 7. Translated by David Constable. Grand Rapids, Michigan: Baker Book House, 1983. Reproduction of *Letters of John Calvin*. Volume 2. Philadelphia: Presbyterian Board of Publication, 1858.

Bouyer, Louis. *The Spirit and Forms of Protestantism*. Translated by A. V. Littledale. Cleveland: Meridian Books, 1964.

Bromiley, G. W., ed. and trans. *Zwingli and Bullinger* (The Library of Christian Classics series). Philadelphia: Westminster Press, 1953.

Bruce, F. F. *The Hard Sayings of Jesus*. Downers Grove, Illinois: Intervarsity Press, 1983.

Calvin, John. *Calvin's Commentaries*. 22 vols. Translated and edited by John Owen. Grand Rapids, Michigan: Baker Book House, 1979. Available online:http://www.ccel .org/c/calvin/comment2/.

Calvin, John. *Institutes of the Christian Religion*. Translated by Henry Beveridge. Grand Rapids, Michigan: Eerdmans Pub. Co., 1995. Available online: http://www.ccel.org/c/calvin/ *Institutes*/*Institutes*.html. See also the 1960 translation listed under McNeill.

Carson. D. A. *Expositor's Bible Commentary: Matthew Mark, Luke*. Vol. 8. Edited by Frank E. Gaebelein. Grand Rapids, Michigan: Zondervan, 1984.

Casciaro, Jose Maria and James Gavigan, eds. *The Navarre Bible: St. Paul's Captivity Epistles*. Dublin: Four Courts Press, 1992.

Chesterton, G. K. *Orthodoxy*. Garden City, New York:
Doubleday Image, 1959. Online at: http://www.dur
.ac.uk/martin.ward/gkc/books/orthodoxy/.

Clarke, Adam [Methodist]. *Commentary on the Bible*. 6
vols. Nashville: Abingdon Press, n.d. Available online:
http://www.godrules.net/library/clarke/clarke.htm.

Conway, Bertrand L. *The Question Box*. Rev. ed. New York:
The Paulist Press, 1929.

Cross, F. L. and E. A. Livingstone, eds. 2nd ed. *The Oxford
Dictionary of the Christian Church*. Oxford: Oxford
University Press, 1983.

Dolan, John P. and James J. Greene, eds. *The Essential Thomas
More*. New York: New American Library, Mentor-Omega,
1967.

Douglas, J. D., ed. *The New Bible Dictionary*. Grand Rapids,
Michigan: Eerdmans Pub. Co., 1962.

Dunn, James D. G. *Unity and Diversity in the New Testament*.
2nd ed. London: SCM Press, 1990.

France, R. T., *Matthew*. Vol. 1 of Tyndale New Testament
Commentaries. Edited by Leon Morris. Leicester, England:
Inter-Varsity Press / Grand Rapids, Michigan: Eerdmans
Pub. Co., 1985.

St. Francis de Sales, *The Catholic Controversy*. Translated by
Henry B. Mackey. Rockford, Illinois: TAN Books, 1989.

Guthrie, D. and J. A. Motyer, eds. *The New Bible Commen-
tary*. 3rd ed. Grand Rapids, Michigan: Eerdmans Pub.
Co., 1970. Reprinted in 1987, as *The Eerdmans Bible
Commentary*.

Hazlitt, William, trans. *Martin Luther: Table-Talk*. Philadelphia:
The Lutheran Publication Society, n.d.

Hendriksen, William. *New Testament Commentary: Exposition
of the Gospel According to Matthew*. Grand Rapids, Michigan:
Baker, 1973.

Henry, Matthew [Presbyterian], *Complete Commentary on the Whole Bible*. Peabody, Massachusetts: Hendrickson Publishers, Inc., 1991. Available online: http://bible .crosswalk.com/*Commentaries*/MatthewHenryComplete/; http://www.studylight.org/com/mhc-com/; http://www .ccel.org/ccel/henry/mhc.html

Herbermann, Charles G., ed. *The Catholic Encyclopedia*. 16 vols. New York: The Encyclopedia Press, 1913. Online at: http://www.newadvent.org/cathen/.

Howard, Thomas, *Evangelical Is Not Enough*. Nashville: Thomas Nelson Publishers, 1984.

Jacobs, C. M., translator, *Works of Martin Luther*. Philadelphia: A. J. Holman Co. and the Castle Press, 1930. Reprinted by Baker Book House, Grand Rapids, Michigan, 1982, six volumes.

Jamieson, Robert [Presbyterian], Andrew R. Fausset [Anglican], and David Brown [Anglican]. *Commentary on the Whole Bible*. Grand Rapids, Michigan: Zondervan, 1961. Available online: http://bible.crosswalk.com/*Commentaries*/ JamiesonFaussetBrown/.

Jurgens, William A., ed. and trans. *The Faith of the Early Fathers*. 3 vols. Collegeville, Minnesota: The Liturgical Press, 1979.

Kelly, J.N.D. *Early Christian Doctrines*. San Francisco: Harper and Row, 1978.

Kittel, Gerhard, *Theological Dictionary of the New Testament*. Edited by Gerhard Kittel and Gerhard Friedrich. Translated and abridged by Geoffrey W. Bromiley. Grand Rapids, Michigan: Eerdmans Pub. Co., 1985.

Knox, Ronald, *The Belief of Catholics*. Garden City, New York: Doubleday Image, 1958.

Lewis, C. S. *The Abolition of Man*. New York: Macmillan, 1947.

Lewis, C. S. *Letters to Malcolm: Chiefly on Prayer*. New York: Harcourt Brace Jovanovich, 1964.

Lindstrom, Harald. *Wesley and Sanctification*. Grand Rapids, Michigan: Francis Asbury Press, 1980.

Luther, Martin. *Luther's Works* (LW). American edition. Edited by Jaroslav Pelikan (vols. 1-30) and Helmut T. Lehmann (vols. 31-55). St. Louis: Concordia Pub. House (vols. 1-30); Philadelphia: Fortress Press (vols. 31-55), 1955.

Luther, Martin. *Large Catechism*, 1529. Translated by Lenker. Minneapolis: Augsburg Publishing House, 1935.

Maier, Gerhard. *The IVP Bible Background Commentary*. Downers Grove, Illinois: InterVarsity Press, 1993.

McNeill, John T., ed. and Ford Lewis Battles, trans. *John Calvin: Institutes of the Christian Religion*. Philadelphia: Westminster Press, 1960.

Merton, Thomas. *Seeds of Contemplation*. New York: Dell Publishing Co., 1949.

Myers, Allen C., ed. *Eerdmans Bible Dictionary*. Grand Rapids, Michigan: Eerdmans Pub. Co., 1987.

Newman, John Henry. *An Essay on the Development of Christian Doctrine*. Notre Dame, Indiana: University of Notre Dame Press, 1989. Available online at: http://www.newmanreader .org/works/development/index.html

Newman, John Henry, Lectures on the Present Position of Catholics in England. London: Longmans, Green and Co., 1918. Available online at: http://www.newmanreader .org/works/england/index.html

Newman, John Henry, Parochial and Plain Sermons. San Francisco: Ignatius Press, 1987. Online at: http://www .newmanreader.org/works/parochial/volume1/index.html (volume I).

O'Connor, Henry. *Luther's Own Statements*. 3rd ed. New York: Benziger Bros., 1884.

Orr, James, ed. *The International Standard Bible Encyclopedia*. 5 vols. Grand Rapids, Michigan: Eerdmans Pub. Co., 1956.

Ott, Ludwig, *Fundamentals of Catholic Dogma*. Translated by Patrick Lynch. Edited by James Canon Bastible. 4th edition in English. Rockford, Illinois: TAN Books, reprinted in 1974.

Packer, J. I. and O. R. Johnston, trans. *The Bondage of the Will*, by Martin Luther (1525). Grand Rapids, Michigan: Fleming H. Revell, 1995.

Robertson, Archibald T. [Baptist]. *Word Pictures in the New Testament*. 6 vols. Nashville: Broadman Press, 1930. Available online: http://bible.crosswalk.com/Commentaries/RobertsonsWordPictures/.

Steinhauser, A. T. W., trans. Martin Luther: The Babylonian Captivity of the Church. From Three Treatises. Rev. ed. Philadelphia: Fortress Press, 1970. Taken from the American edition of Luther's Works, edited by Jaroslav Pelikan (see under Luther), vols. 31, 36, 44.

Strong, Augustus Hopkins. Systematic Theology. Westwood, New Jersey: Fleming H. Revell Co., 1907.

Svendsen, Eric D., *Who Is My Mother?* Amityville, New York: Calvary Press, 2001.

Tappert, Theodore G., trans. and ed. *The Book of Concord*. St. Louis: Concordia Publishing House, 1959.

Thayer, Joseph H. *Greek-English Lexicon of the New Testament*. Grand Rapids, Michigan: Baker Book House, 1977.

Tozer, A. W. *A Treasury of A. W. Tozer*. Grand Rapids, Michigan: Baker Book House, 1980.

Vincent, Marvin R. *Word Studies in the New Testament*. 4 vols. Grand Rapids, Michigan: Eerdmans Pub. Co., 1946.

Vine, W. E. *An Expository Dictionary of New Testament Words*. Old Tappan, New Jersey: Fleming H. Revell Co., 1940.

Wendel, François. *Calvin: Origins and Development of His Religious Thought*. Translated by Philip Mairet. New York: Harper and Row, 1963.

Wesley, John [founder of Methodism]. *Explanatory Notes on the New Testament*, 1766. London: Epworth, 1958. Available online: http://bible.crosswalk.com/*Commentaries*/WesleysExplanatoryNotes/.

White, James R. *The Roman Catholic Controversy*. Minneapolis: Bethany House Publishers, 1996.

Williams, George H. and Angel M. Mergal, eds. *Spiritual and Anabaptist Writers*. Philadelphia: Westminster Press, 1957.

Biographical Note

Dave Armstrong

Dave Armstrong is a Catholic writer, apologist, and evangelist who has been actively proclaiming and defending Christianity for more than twenty years. Formerly a campus missionary, as a Protestant, Armstrong was received into the Catholic Church in 1991 by the late, well-known catechist and theologian Fr. John A. Hardon, S.J.

Armstrong's conversion story appeared in the bestselling book *Surprised by Truth* and his articles have been published in a number of Catholic periodicals, including *The Catholic Answer*, *This Rock*, *Envoy*, *Hands On Apologetics*, *The Coming Home Journal*, and *The Latin Mass*. His apologetic and writing apostolate was the subject of a feature article in the May 2002 issue of *Envoy*. Armstrong is the author of the books *A Biblical Defense of Catholicism* and *More Biblical Evidence for Catholicism* and of forty-four apologetics articles in *The Catholic Answer Bible*.

His website, *Biblical Evidence for Catholicism* (www.biblicalcatholic .com), online since March 1997, received the 1998 Catholic Website of the Year award from *Envoy*, which also nominated Armstrong himself for Best New Evangelist.

Armstrong and his wife, Judy, and their four children live near Detroit, Michigan.

Sophia Institute Press®